The
TEST

INCREDIBLE PROOF OF
THE AFTERLIFE

STÉPHANE ALLIX
Translated by Grace McQuillan

Helios
press

Copyright © 2018 by Stéphane Allix

Original title: Le Test
© Editions Albin Michel, Paris 2015

Helios books may be purchased in bulk at special discounts for sales promotion, corporate gifts, fund-raising, or educational purposes. Special editions can also be created to specifications. For details, contact the Special Sales Department, Skyhorse Publishing, 307 West 36th Street, 11th Floor, New York, NY 10018 or info@skyhorsepublishing.com.

Helios Press is an imprint of Skyhorse Publishing, Inc.®, a Delaware corporation.

Visit our website at www.skyhorsepublishing.com.

10 9 8 7 6 5 4 3 2 1

Library of Congress Cataloging-in-Publication Data

Names: Allix, Stephane, author.
Title: The test : incredible proof of the afterlife / Stephane Allix ;
    translated by Grace McQuillan.
Other titles: Test. English
Description: New York, New York : Helios Press, an imprint of Skyhorse
    Publishing, Inc., 2018.
Identifiers: LCCN 2018003157 (print) | LCCN 2018014419 (ebook) | ISBN
    9781510729377 (eBook) | ISBN 9781510729360 (pbk. : alk. paper)
Subjects: LCSH: Mediums--Interviews. | Future life. | Spiritualism.
Classification: LCC BF1311.F8 (ebook) | LCC BF1311.F8 A4513 2018
(print) |
    DDC 133.9/1--dc23
LC record available at https://lccn.loc.gov/2018003157

Paperback ISBN: 978-1-5107-2936-0
eBook ISBN: 978-1-5107-2937-7

Cover design by Jane Sheppard
Cover illustration by iStockphoto

Printed in the United States of America

Contents

"Nothing is more illuminating than the beautiful death of a loved one."
—Michka

Introduction

When my father passed away, I placed four objects
    in his casket. I spoke about it to no one. I then
    interviewed mediums who claimed to be able to
    communicate with the dead.
Would they discover what the objects were?
This is the test.

My father, Jean-Pierre Allix, passed away on June 16, 2013, at the age of eighty-five. He was an admirable father; I loved him and still do. He taught me to be a man whose word and sense of honor meant more than anything else. He encouraged me to become a person who expected as much from myself as I did from other people and to be proud of my heritage. He taught me to be curious, to know how to use my best judgment, but also to listen without judging too quickly. He showed me by his example that life is astonishing, and that it is precisely this ability to be astonished, whatever one's age, that saves us from despair. He showed me how to watch, read, understand, and search. He introduced me to Tolstoy, Flaubert, and Stendhal, and he inculcated in me the importance of constructing sentences that mean something but that are also pleasant to read. "A text is music," he used to say.

As you read what follows, you will better understand why I think my father is far more than the mere subject of a peculiar experiment, namely the test I put forward to six mediums, two men and four women. He is my partner, the invisible but central character in this book, to which he contributed at times with difficulty, often with emotion, and even, at certain moments, with humor.

When he was alive, we had spoken about death on several occasions; in 2001, I had lost a brother, and he a son, in an accident in Afghanistan, and the subject was ever present in my family. We had both mentioned how interesting it would be, after his death, to try and undertake this research together.

The day of his burial, I was alone in the room at the funeral parlor. A few minutes before the casket would be closed and sealed, I took four objects along with a little note and hid them under the fabric covering his corpse, out of sight. From that moment and until the casket was closed, I remained next to it to reassure myself that no one could see the objects concealed against his body. I am also absolutely certain to have been, until today, the only person aware of the presence of those objects in his casket.

On that Saturday morning of June 22, 2013, I left the following things next to my father:

- a long, thin paintbrush,
- a tube of white acrylic paint,
- his compass,
- a paperback copy of *The Tartar Steppe* by Dino Buzzati, one of his favorite books,
- and a small note slipped inside an ecru-colored envelope.

I took the time to photograph each object just before putting it into the casket. Then, I spoke to my father, looking at the empty space above him rather than at his body. I explained to him what I was doing, and that his task would consist of telling the mediums what the objects were. A little over a year later, I asked several mediums if they would be willing to participate in a small experiment, though I remained very evasive as to what the subject of this experiment was.

Science and mediumship

Can we really communicate with the dead? Some claim it is possible and even practice it as a profession. A certain number among them are not charlatans. So who are they? The objective of this test is to investigate six mediums known for their reliability, their honesty, and, of course, their well-recognized abilities.

The number of people who use the ability to communicate with the beyond professionally is greater than we might imagine. Thousands of people consult with them, but few talk about it.

What are the challenges of mediumship? Is there material to be probed? Are these abilities real? Is this a phenomenon of society that we can reduce to a kind of swindle, unconscious on the part of certain mediums, but completely conscious for other charlatans? Are we dealing with a collective illusion? A form of autosuggestion in people who are unable to overcome the reality of loss? Or are we talking about real communication with the afterlife? For those who practice it, is it a gift or a curse? A vocation or an illusion?

Through the six encounters I am offering you, and the six test séances that I will attend, I am going to attempt to answer all of these questions with thoroughness and objectivity.

Mediums claim that the deceased are present beside them—they see them, feel them, speak with them—and that they receive information simply because the deceased are whispering in their ear. You will discover that upon analysis, the data shows that this idea is plausible: an aspect of our personality or our identity could continue to exist after physical death in a form capable of communicating with a medium.

Life after death is, today, a rational hypothesis. Scientific research conducted on mediumship has allowed this to be confirmed.

A medium is a person who, by connecting with one or several deceased people, obtains information, sometimes of an intimate nature, about a person they are meeting for the first time in their lives. This is, in fact, one of the most mysterious things about mediumship, because to date no explanation exists that would allow us to determine in a conventional way how such a thing is possible.

When the medium finds themself in front of a client they don't know, whom they are usually seeing for the first time, they are able to deliver a fair amount of more or less significant factual information, claiming to receive it from people who have passed away. The question is, where does this information come from? Research has been conducted over several decades, notably by researchers such as Gary E. Schwartz[1] and, more recently, Julie Beischel[2] of the Windbridge Institute. This research analyzes the nature of information that mediums are capable of obtaining while under strictly controlled conditions.

The first two conventional ways to obtain information about a person we don't know are fraud or deception. In these cases, the medium would have acquired information about the target subject, the deceased person, beforehand. Julie Beischel explains that her research protocol eliminates this

---

1   Gary E. Schwartz, *The Afterlife Experiments*, Atria Books, 2002.
2   Julie Beischel, *Among Mediums: A Scientist's Quest for Answers*, Windbridge Institute, LLC, 2013.

possibility since the medium has only the first name of the deceased person throughout the entire experiment. Another conventional explanation, she says, is cold reading, when the medium uses visual or auditory clues that they perceive in the client in order to present information that resonates. This is also called "mentalism." In order to guard against this, in Beischel's experiments, the person playing the role of the client is not physically present in the same room as the medium, and the person who leads the experiment also knows nothing about the subject or any potential deceased individuals associated with that person. A final possible explanation: the information provided by the medium is so general that it could be applied to anybody. To eliminate this last possibility, Beischel asks the medium to provide four specific facts about the deceased: physical description, personality, pastimes or activities, and cause of death.

The results obtained throughout many successive experiments allow us to definitively put aside conventional explanations such as fraud, directive questioning, or suggestibility. With these protocols, researchers like Julie Beischel and Gary Schwartz have eliminated every conventional explanation.

So how do mediums obtain information about people, living and dead, whom they know nothing about? Researchers find themselves faced with two hypotheses that might account for their results: either the mediums are really communicating with the deceased, or there is a form of telepathy at work—this explanation in itself is already fairly extraordinary. According to this second hypothesis, the medium would be capable of *reading into* the spirit of the person coming to consult them. They would not speak to a spirit, but would obtain information by digging into the head of the person facing them, who knows this information.

However, the evidence seems to show that this form of telepathy is a passive act, with the medium receiving images and flashes, whereas in communications with the dead, mediums describe actual interactive conversations. Still more decisive is the fact that in many cases the information delivered by the medium is unknown to the person who enters the experiment as a client. As Gary Schwartz specifies, "We often get people the subject knows but wasn't expecting to hear from. Other times, we get information that the subject believes is false or didn't know about and then finds out later to be true."

This is rather baffling, because a true telepathic flash cannot contradict what the person is thinking. Moreover, as Julie Beischel underlines, psychic readings are part of the practice of numerous mediums. They are very capable, they say, of making the distinction between telepathy and communication with a deceased person: the feelings associated with each situation are different. It is also something they have experienced since childhood. We are going to explore this in greater detail later.

Thus, the scientific approach of mediumship allows us to conclude that, in Beischel's words, "the receiving of abnormal information is a fact but we cannot determine where it arises from. The data supports the idea of a survival of the consciousness, of a life after death. An aspect of our personality or of our identity continues to exist after physical death in a form capable of communicating with a medium. The data also reinforces other hypotheses unrelated to the survival of the consciousness: clairvoyance, telepathy, or precognition would allow mediums to acquire information without communicating with the dead. However, now that we have started working on the experience of mediums, we are now inclined to think that the survival of the consciousness is the explanation most supported by the data."

By virtue of all the research that has been done and that I my-self have conducted in recent years,[3] life after death is today, in my view, more than a solid hypothesis. For over ten years I have been carrying out my investigation across the world, meeting researchers, physicians, men, women, and children who have had incredible experiences of contact with the de-ceased. I have been working and rubbing shoulders with me-diums for years. All this time I have remained in my role as a thorough and objective journalist. It is precisely this approach that has led me to recognize the proof before me today: death is not the end of life.

With this book I also intend to contribute to the debate by bringing forth indisputable evidence that you will discover in these pages. But beyond simply wanting to *prove* that life continues after death, I have hoped to explore how this com-munication between two worlds, *between the living and the dead*, is established. I questioned the mediums relentlessly: what happens to us when our body vanishes into dust? What happens to our consciousness after death? For we continue to be, of this today I am certain. But what is the nature of our being? Are we exactly the same person we were during our lifetime on earth? Or does our personhood evolve? What happens during the first weeks following our death? Where do we go? Who do we meet?

Who is the being my father became after his death, who communicated with me?

---

3   Stéphane Allix, *La mort n'est pas une terre étrangère*, Albin Michel, 2011, J'ai Lu, 2014; *Enquêtes extraordinaires*, seasons 1 and 2, *Les Signes de l'au-delà*, and *Ils communiquent avec les morts*, documen-taries directed by Natacha Calestrémé et al., DVD, Éd. Montpar-nasse, 2011 and 2014.

I invite you to discover what months of investigation have permitted me to understand. It is dizzying. Each one of the six chapters to follow is the portrait of a medium and presents, in its entirety, the test séance conducted with him or her. I have never gone as far in any of my interviews as I did in these. They shed an unparalleled light on the end of life, death, the afterlife, and communication with the dead. In the final chapter, psychiatrist Christophe Fauré, a specialist in caring for people at the end of life, discusses the specific features of the path of grief and offers us some kind advice regarding death and mediumship.

Writing this book changed my life. Perhaps it will change yours.

Henry

I am feeling very apprehensive about this séance. I have known Henry Vignaud for years, and there is a true friendship between us. I met him for the first time in November 2006 to test him, even back then, with a photo of my brother Thomas, who had died five years earlier in Afghanistan. The result of that first séance was impressive.[4] He knew nothing about me, yet there is no doubt in my mind that Henry communicated with my brother that day.

As far as doubts, though, I still had my fair share. I came out of the small apartment where we had met feeling torn between astonishment and resistance. Astonishment at the fact that he had given me an incredible number of very specific details about my brother, his life, his personality, the particular circumstances of his death, etc., details that he could not, in total objectivity, have gotten from anyone except my brother himself, who had been dead for five years! And resistance because what the evidence was telling me—that my brother had spoken to me *after his death*—was something my mind was not yet ready to accept.

This resistance is tenacious, and clings onto the smallest doubt, taking advantage of the slightest opportunity it

---

4   Stéphane Allix, *La mort n'est pas une terre étrangère*, Albin Michel, 2011, J'ai Lu, 2014.

is given. On that day in November 2006, for example, what bothered me most was that at no point had Henry ever said that my brother's name was Thomas. He had described in detail the way Thomas had died in a car accident, his wound to the head, the place where it had happened, but he had not said his name. This seemed paradoxical. Why, since Henry claimed that he was with us in the room, didn't my brother simply say, with me in mind, "Uh, hey, tell him my name is Thomas"? This seemed both incomprehensible and illogical to me, and this small annoyance diminished the completely unexplained fact that Henry had also given me a great deal of *other true information.*

I have since discovered the reason for this apparent contradiction, and it is one of the things that is so important for me to explore with the six mediums who have agreed to take part in my proposed test. In very basic terms—this point is crucial, and we will come back to it throughout this book—the part of a medium's brain that *perceives* the words, images, and information on behalf of the deceased is not the same as the part of the brain that *verbalizes* this information to the living person who has come to see them. Researcher Julie Beischel explained this to me during an interview I had with her in Tucson, Arizona, a few years ago: "Names and dates pose a problem for many mediums. I think this is because this kind of information depends on the left brain. A name is a label, and numbers and labels are managed by the left hemisphere of the brain. We think that mediumship is a process that occurs primarily via the right brain. Elements that are normally filtered by our left brain are therefore more difficult to perceive and interpret."

A parallel can be made to the moment a person first wakes up. In that instant, it is possible that you retain the last dream you just had. It is there, you can feel it, the memory

of it is ingrained in you with all of its power and its evoca-
tions. But you move or stretch, and before you even get up it
has withered away. Curiously, when you try to make a note
of it by writing it down, or by telling your spouse about it,
the words you use actually *destroy* a part of the dream. By
saying it or by putting it down in writing, you are reducing
it to words. It reconstructs itself. It almost becomes something else. In fact, you have just passed from the right brain,
which dreams, to the left brain, which is trying to describe
the dream. Things get stuck. You still hold the vague sensation of fragments of the dream: there was more of a . . .
there's something there you can't quite remember . . . the
color was . . . how to put this? No, despite your efforts, you
are not able to find the words. A medium's experience, as we
are going to find out, is a little like that: during a séance they
must both remain in the dream, that delicate space of fragile
perceptions where they are in contact with the deceased, and
tell you what is happening with words. The ability to do this
permanent back-and-forth without altering one's perceptions
is the secret to being a good medium.

As I drive through Paris toward the neighborhood where
Henry lives, I wonder how our friendship might affect this
interview. Will the trust we have in each other make the test
less stressful for him? Or, on the contrary, will the stakes of the
experiment paralyze him? Stress is an important factor whenever a person has to tune into their subtle senses, which are by
definition tenuous and very fragile. These delicate perceptions,
which we might suppose are related to intuition or a sixth sense,
are directly affected by the slightest hint of emotion. And stress,
the fear of *not succeeding*, is an enormous emotion. None of the
mediums participating in this test will be spared from this.

In spite of our long friendship, Henry never met my father, and on the off chance that he has been informed about

his death one year ago, he knows nothing else about him. Nothing about the circumstances of his death, and obviously nothing about the experiment I undertook in secret at the funeral parlor where his casket was sealed. But strangely, at no moment will Henry mention that it is my father we will be making contact with, though, as you will see, that is exactly the person who shows up.

As usual, I leave early, worried about having trouble finding parking. I head toward the southern part of Paris, still north of the Place d'Italie. As usual, I quickly find a parking spot a few minutes' walk from Henry's place. I'm impatient. Waiting until the scheduled meeting time, I stay sitting behind the steering wheel, in the warmth. As I've been doing for several days, I take advantage of the time to speak out loud to my father and to all the other deceased people in my family who might be able to hear me in the invisible world. I ask them for help. Help with this book. Help for Papa, so that he is able to tell Henry what I put inside his casket. As I'm talking out loud inside my car, I suddenly think that for one of the objects—the book by Dino Buzzati, *The Tartar Steppe*—it's going to be nearly impossible for a medium to *understand* the title, even if Papa gives it to him, when even a simple first name is so hard to obtain. Will one of the six mediums even be able to name the book? I'm still far from being able to imagine that in a little over an hour, right in the middle of the séance, an extraordinary synchronicity will occur when my father finds a solution.

I enter an apartment with drawn curtains. Henry is smiling and joyful, as he always is. He is a man who always has a cheerful way about him even when life is bothering him. He looks like he is doing well and waves me into the living room, which serves as his consultation area. It is a simple room with a small table placed at an angle to the wall. The room smells of cigarettes. I can sense at once that he is also very apprehensive about this moment. He informs me that he has not done a consultation in a long time. Between family obligations and a terrible case of bronchitis, the séance he will perform with me will be his first in several weeks. Ouch! Does an unused medium get rusty?

It is already dim but he closes the shutters, plunging the room into darkness. Henry likes to be in the dark when he works. To start, I don't give him any direction or photo to see who will spontaneously appear. Who are the deceased people around me who would like to make themselves heard?

Henry sits down behind his small table cluttered with various papers, religious images, a small gold icon depicting Padre Pio (famous for his stigmata and canonized in 2002), and an ashtray, and hides his face behind his hands to focus. I am sitting across from him, concentrating and waiting. The minutes spread into a silence that is only punctuated with a few fits of coughing. Bronchitis and cigarettes don't make a good pair. I wonder how he can concentrate when he's coughing like that. And then, softly, out it comes.

"Do you often light candles?" he asks me.

I find it funny that he's asking me a question like this because just this very morning, before coming to our meeting, I lit one, which I never do. In front of the flame, I addressed Papa. On the other hand, my wife Natacha offers a silent prayer to her loved ones while lighting a candle almost daily.

"Me, no, but Natacha does it often."

"There is spiritual appreciation for the candles that are lit regularly for several deceased people, by you or Natacha, it's the same thing."

"I actually did that this morning before I came."

"There is appreciation for that light . . . I've been seeing this for a little while, even earlier before we started."

After this preamble, silence sets in again. Henry is concentrating, his face in his hands.

"I am sensing the vague presence of the face of someone who has died, someone who had a beard, a kind of goatee, the kind that quite a few people had at one time."

"That doesn't ring a bell for me."

Right as I'm saying this, as Henry makes reference to a distant time, I suddenly think of my great-grandfather, Georges, who had a goatee and mustache. I don't say anything, though, because without more details on his end, what Henry said is too vague. More time goes by.

"Paul, does that mean anything to you? Or Jean-Paul?"

"Yes."

"Is it Paul or Jean-Paul? I heard Paul but it could be Jean-Paul."

"It's Paul."

"Deceased? Because he's right up there."

"Yes."

"He's trying to show me different devices; they almost look like surgical devices, from an operating room. Yes, that's it; either this person underwent surgery, or this operation had consequences for his earthly departure . . . either way he was operated on before leaving . . . An operation was necessary and he left just afterwards. This doesn't mean anything to you?"

One of the most painful episodes in the life of my father's mother, Lise, was the death of her big brother Paul. He was reported missing at the age of thirty-one on February 18, 1915, during the violent fighting that took place in the hamlet of Beauséjour in Champagne-Ardenne. The villages in that part of the Marne were entirely destroyed; only the hamlet was never rebuilt. The memory of Paul's disappearance has marked the family ever since.

How can a person *disappear* on a battlefield? I can't imagine what that means. We don't know anything about the exact circumstances of his death. "Declared missing" means that no trace of his remains had been found, so it is hardly likely that he had been wounded, undergone surgery, and then died during the operation. Why would he then have been declared missing? Doubtful, I remain evasive and don't mention any of this to Henry. He carries on. Things become unsettling.

"This man is here, I can see him. It seems he had stomach problems. Do you know him?"

"I don't know. Are you talking about Paul?"

"It seems like it . . . no, hold on. Someone else had serious stomach problems and was operated on. It's not Paul."

It would seem that several people are coming forward and that the pieces of information Henry is capturing are superimposing themselves on one another. I am struck by the appearance of this Paul, someone whose disappearance from our family had overwhelmed my grandmother, but also by the mention of a man with stomach problems whose operation led to death. This was exactly what my father suffered from!

He had a problem in his stomach, ascites, meaning that his belly was extremely swollen, filling with water. During the last months of his life, he underwent several puncturing procedures at the hospital. With the help of a large needle, several gallons of water were removed from his body. The night before his death, a final puncture to a body that was already profoundly weakened had taken his remaining strength, and he slipped into unconsciousness, dying the next day. This man who had appeared at the same time as Paul, who "had serious stomach problems," who "was operated on before leaving," and whose operation "had consequences for his earthly departure" was definitely my father! And Paul was his uncle.

Henry then returns to Paul with new information, just as extraordinary.

"Paul was very sad before leaving, I can see that his eyes are shining . . . There is the letter 'F' coming up . . . a first name, a last name?"

Being sad to leave, nothing original there, but the letter F! Paul called himself Lafitte. Am I being too hasty putting the pieces together? But still, here were several things right in a row that fit together very well: Paul F, for Paul Lafitte, the man who left just after a stomach operation, which is exactly what happened to my father, Paul's nephew. I stay quiet and keep all of this to myself for now.

The séance continues with long silences once again. Since I'm not leading him anywhere, I get the feeling that Henry is receiving a lot of brief images: for example, he sees me as a child, going very quickly up the stairs; well, when I was a child we lived on the sixth floor of a building on Rue Gay-Lussac in Paris, and I used to run up the stairs. He describes fairly exactly what I was like in those days. I ask him to put into words everything that comes to his mind, without giving him any extra details.

"Did you ever keep a revolver or rifle bullet in your house?" he asks me suddenly.

"Yes."

"Because I'm being shown the bullet with fingertips, I don't know why."

In my house I have several Kalashnikov bullets brought back from my trips to Afghanistan, bullets I had taken the powder out of. But why has this been brought up? I sense some agitation on the side of the dead: they're trying to show me things that will serve as reminders, things that have something to do with other times, or with different people in my family, but everything is coming a bit frenetically and out of order. If I helped Henry, this would probably allow him to concentrate better on this person or that person on the other side, on one thing versus another, but first I still want to observe what happens when the medium receives everything, with no targeting of one dead person in particular.

This is what is unique during a séance of mediumship, and what can sometimes be a way for the medium to claim to have communicated with the dead while they are merely formulating one vague but ordinary thing after another: we are the ones who will give meaning to things that do not have any. I am very attentive to this point, but at the same time I am very aware that staying quiet makes Henry's task more arduous, even though it preserves a necessary objectivity. Still, that man with a stomach problem is my father, I'm convinced, just as I am equally aware that without having confirmation from me, Henry has not "held onto" this soul, has not focused on it, and is continuing to let its spirit roam the subtle world.

"In your family, at one time, there wasn't someone who had a snake? This is bizarre."

"Yes, me."

I adored those animals and had kept some in a terrarium, but my brother Thomas, who died in April 2001, was also a huge fan of snakes and had also kept several in his bedroom.

"You?" Henry sounds surprised. "I see a snake moving in front of me . . . You had a snake?"

"Yes, my brother did too, actually."

"Ah . . . it's strange, I saw the snake in front of me, crawling on top of the table."

This confirms it, Henry is not having any trouble—he's receiving things. One must imagine that he is observing a somewhat evanescent crowd—an invisible crowd, for me—in which every person is waving to him at the same time. My father is in the middle of this crowd, and it seems that as long we work blindly, he will not be in a position to make himself more noticeable to Henry amid the other spirits. Yes, before Henry's "eyes of the soul" is an indistinct crowd of spirits. I am really complicating things for him by staying silent.

We are friends, he knows my history, and in the past he has captured my brother several times with remarkable precision. I also have no doubts about his abilities. In spite of everything, this consultation generates a certain apprehension in me, and this must not be helpful in what should be a completely relaxed situation. Also, since he knows the details of my brother's death, I sense that even if he sees Thomas in this crowd, he won't tell me about it and will self-censor himself in a way.

We move onto the second step; I don't want him to exhaust himself with this blind exercise without giving him a chance to show me once more what he is capable of. I take out the photo of my father and place it on the table without telling him who it is. Instantly, I observe the effect of this image's presence, which Henry only looks at for two seconds before taking it and placing it on his forehead, his eyes still closed. It's as if suddenly in the middle of the great maelstrom of invisible forces an instantaneous connection has just formed between the man in the photo, who has been present around us among so many other people since we started, and Henry. A direct link, free from all of that crosstalk brought about by the presence of the other deceased around him. So many singular beings, with their requests, their images, their own feelings . . .

Will my father be able to express himself more clearly? Will he be able to tell Henry what I'm expecting?

How does one become a medium? When he is asked this question, Henry Vignaud always mentions his earliest memory. He is seven years old when he sees for the first time a hanged man in one of the rooms in the house where he is living. He is the only one in his family to see this scene. From his bedroom, he can make out very clearly the shape of a man hanging from a rope. This vision is becoming more and more frequent, and his parents are intrigued by it (it is not until much later that they will be astonished to discover that the former owner had hung himself in the exact spot where Henry saw him).

Henry has this vision for years, until the family moves. When he is asked to describe it, he talks about it more as a frozen image than something that is alive. Much later he will discover that it was not a spirit, but a memory of what had happened in the house. Like a recording, a piece of film that replayed itself over and over. Why did he pick up on it? He has no idea, but he explains that tragic deaths like this man's are accompanied by great pain, and this is probably what leaves an imprint on a place, the imprint of someone truly present to the eyes of a young child, as he was then: a man, head lowered, hanging at the end of a rope. Even though it recurs fairly frequently, he fortunately does not see this image every day. When it does appear, he snuggles beneath the covers and looks, all the same, through a small hole in the sheets. At first he is so frightened. Then, with time, in a certain way, he becomes used to it, as much as one can become used to something like that.

The vision of this mysterious and silent hanging man is followed by visions that are more *alive*. Over the years, the unexplained phenomena multiply. Henry feels things coming toward him, appearing in his bedroom. He talks about curls of smoke, of materializations of unknown faces. These faces emerge before his eyes, sometimes appearing against a backdrop, a landscape that seems to be linked to their existence. Unlike the hanging man, Henry now has the sensation that they are completely alive and showing him scenes from their lives. He does not really hear voices, but he has the feeling of becoming a kind of magnet for these beings.

Despite his young age, Henry wonders if it has to do with spirits, people who are coming to see him. In retrospect, today he thinks they were appearing on purpose with the objective of encouraging his awakening of that awareness, for since his birth, Henry has demonstrated a particular kind of sensitivity. In his childhood years, it was a door that opened toward an unknown dimension.

He lives these years as if in spiritual preparation. It is directed and voluntary, for the people who come are not spirits from his family appearing in a kind of parasitic way with specific demands. No, back then Henry was dealing with spirits totally unknown to him, which seemed to be moved by a very particular intention.

He is lucky enough to be able to speak freely about it with his sisters and his mother at first, then to other loved ones and even his buddies at school, though the reception is sometimes quite different, depending on the person. Before he encountered the skeptical eyes and judgements of others, what he was experiencing had seemed normal to him; he thought that everyone saw what he saw. But the first instances of teasing and the cutting remarks make him wonder if something is wrong with him. Yet despite the sometimes relentless judgement, Henry feels deep down that he is experiencing real things. He is a balanced child and of sound mind.

Even though in the beginning these experiences some-times frightened him, he realizes that he never had the feel-ing of being attacked. Little by little, he becomes familiar with the existence of these other dimensions. This reality re-veals itself naturally to him in the privacy of the small village where he lives, far away from everything, without access to a single book on these subjects. The television never mentions it. More than the fear or the doubt, this is what is hardest for him: not having access to any information. He experiences these phenomena without knowing what they are. Only one thing is certain: they are alive, and real.

Henry enters adolescence through moments that are sometimes very intense. These experiences might happen every day, even several times a night, but then fifteen days may go by, even three weeks, with nothing happening. With adolescence, certain kinds of flashes begin to ap-pear. He picks up on an event, something confirmed by the person facing him—members of his family, or friends at school. He also perceives things that are going to hap-pen. At school, people start calling him the Sorcerer. Un-derstanding that he is the only one experiencing things like this does not make him doubtful for one moment. He no longer asks himself whether his imagination is playing tricks on him. No, it's too invasive, too real, too alive for that. Finally, his parents discover that a man had really hung himself in their house where Henry had seen him. This confirms for him that his perceptions are not the fruits of his imagination.

Henry talks with much goodwill about the way these ap-paritions trained him. The intuitive understanding that he forges from these phenomena and the role they play in his awakening make him more and more confident: an outside will is intervening.

Throughout his entire childhood, Henry is imbued with a kind of confidence. He knows that his visions are opening another dimension to him, but a true initiation begins when his out of body experiences make their debut. In fact, since the age of sixteen, he has experienced signs of *discorporation*, of becoming removed from his physical body.

Like many paranormal experiences that Henry still has today, these new experiences take place in the minutes following the moment he falls asleep. The first few times, he recalls, he has the sensation that the bottom of his body is lifting up—not his physical legs, but *another body*—while the top does not move. Other times, it is the top of the body that will lift up, ready to leave, but the bottom part will not move. Then he has the desire to leave his body, feeling a surge of energy and realizing that something is happening, but in the end nothing comes of it. This lasts for months and months, and then one day, abruptly, he finds himself on all fours next to his bed. Nothing shocking about that, until he notices that his body is still in the bed while *he* is on all fours next to it. Surprised, he becomes afraid and immediately finds himself back in his physical body. Another time, he sees himself sitting on the edge of his bed, then standing up, and when he goes to turn on the light, his hand passes through the switch and the wall. It is his astral body that has just gotten up, without him realizing it. As he turns around, he sees his physical body and feels a strange sensation. Fear carries him away again.

It takes whole months for him to slowly become accustomed to these experiences. With no willingness on his part—he's not trying to leave his body—these experiences happen, just like that. And there is a constant subtle intuition that has inhabited him since childhood: that he is undergoing a kind of training. When the fear becomes more manageable over time, he discovers that at the instant when the physical sensations that characterize the beginning of the experience manifest themselves, *they* are calling him. A mysterious voice murmurs to him: "Come." It is the voice of his guide, which he will not understand until much later.

Reassured by what he believes to be pleasant and protective spiritual forces, he then allows himself to leave. Guided by a benevolent voice, he soon increases the voyages out of his body, a body that rests obediently in his bed while this happens. Despite the greater and greater frequency of his astral voyages, Henry is never able to choose to go to a specific location, to see his mother, for example. When he finds himself outside his body, his will is blocked and *they* show him things.

Could these be dreams, insofar as his experiences happen when he is in bed? Most of the time, in fact, he is lying down, but the clarity and the force of these experiences removes every doubt: this has nothing to do with dreaming. This confidence inhabits him even before these experiences begin happening in the light of day, such as the time when, as an adult, he leaves his body . . . while in the supermarket.

Henry is shopping with friends, including medium Nicole Leprince. Suddenly, as he is pushing his cart through the aisles, looking for what he needs to make a nice dinner, he starts to feel strange, really strange. He stops so he can pay more attention to his perceptions. Perhaps he is picking up on an energy that belongs to his surroundings in this moment, or the energy of someone around him, a spirit, even. As a young adult, he has become used to these kinds of spontaneous perceptions. He still has a hard time describing them; it would be like an energy around him. In any case, on that day he leaves his body, is lifted high above the aisles, and observes from his new viewpoint the people busy with their shopping, his friends, and . . . translucent silhouettes with vague shapes, which he realizes are spirits swarming among the living people.

While this is happening, his frozen body remains standing, his hands on the cart, his head elsewhere, both literally and figuratively, as if he is absorbed in his thoughts. In that instant, Henry finds himself both physically present and in another reality, observing from above. His friend Nicole understands what is happening and takes him by the arm, saying, "Henry, come back to us . . ." Henry notices a hubbub around him, but he hears his friend's call. And she brings him back. Very gently.

This discorporation was probably accidental, and in that way different from all the others. It did not seem voluntary, though leaving his body in the store was very instructive. That day he becomes physically aware of the extent to which we are living constantly surrounded by spirits. Henry knows this in an abstract manner at the time, but to see it with his own eyes, to observe that we are surrounded, even infested by such an abundance of the souls of the dead, surprises him. He could never have imagined it like this. He does not know if the dead in the supermarket were the loved ones of people who were shopping. He will discover later that at times souls will pollute the environment of a living person or a place. Certain people attract strange energies, parasitic souls. As a medium, he himself sometimes feels emptied of his energy by a deceased person.

Henry describes this out of body experience in the middle of the supermarket as an accident, quite unlike the majority of the experiences he had beginning at a young age. He is now profoundly convinced of this because someone came to him to confirm it.

All throughout his childhood, the way other people considered him led Henry to feel more and more different from everyone else, even though at the beginning everything seemed normal to him. Little by little he became aware that he was capable of seeing things that other people didn't. He was confronted by forces and entities that had their own life. But during adolescence, during his out of body experiences, he began to hear the voice of a being who would introduce itself to him as his guide. With this person, he began to live a new phase in his apprenticeship.

Now all fear is gone, he knows he is safe. When his guide tells him, "Come," he cannot resist, it's impossible. He struggles to explain it these days. Is it a reassuring voice? A voice that invades his entire being, submerging him in such peace. As if their souls recognized one another, and as if this guide was someone he had always known. Once he leaves with the guide, Henry knows he is not in danger, even if it is difficult to say where he goes. He doesn't really go anywhere, such as another place some distance away; rather, he is swept away into planes of light that are meant to make him directly aware of a few very specific things. For example, one time his guide shows Henry a person who has just died, someone he doesn't know. The guide wants Henry to observe the spirits who are busying themselves around this person. He observes the deceased person, the other spirits around him, beings of light; he doesn't really know what to call them. That day his guide makes him realize that the dead man does not know that he is dead, as often happens, and that in reality he is just beginning to understand.

I am surprised to learn that though this guide was so present during his life, Henry only saw him once. During each of their escapades, when he invites him to follow, Henry feels his presence next to him but never sees him. Sometimes only an arm materializes, the guide staying behind Henry. He feels enveloped by the guide's power, and his force presses him onward. Henry is unable to imagine that this power could have come from within himself. It comes from somewhere else, and that outside force, the help of his guide, plays a large role in the ease with which he leaves his body. Henry frees himself from physical matter and, enveloped by this energy, he is propelled somewhere else. But still, he never sees him.

Except one time: there is the usual "Come," and immediately afterward Henry is literally grabbed and finds himself face to face with a being in a dimension where other evanescent beings are also present. Henry then experiences a force of light and extraordinary love and peace. In this unforgettable experience, before these fabulous beings, he himself is filled with light and sees him, his guide, for the first and last time in his life.

Words can hardly transcribe these kinds of experiences. Henry speaks of a being of incredible beauty. His face is human, and radiates with an indescribable light. That day, he gives Henry a little smile, tilting his head; a kind of gentle confirmation that it is indeed he who has been guiding him all this time. And that's it. Since that day, Henry has known in his heart and every one of his cells who the spirit is that accompanies and helps him.

When he is in consultation, in contact with the dead, the guide sometimes intervenes and plays the role of an intermediary between the dead and the living, though this isn't always the case. Henry defines him more as a protective and loving being who helps him to evolve and focus himself. There is never any discussion between them. It is only on his initiative that the guide addresses Henry. One sentence or two and nothing more. With love and sometimes with reprimands, the way a parent might do with their child.

One of the most significant recommendations that the guide has given Henry was that he decide to make mediumship his career. As astonishing as this may seem, Henry did not want to.

He receives the order when he is nineteen. At the time it is given first by his guide. A voice forcing itself upon him, with no doubt about its source. The message is as follows: "Later on you will have thousands of souls to support, and in particular parents who have lost their children." At nineteen, Henry doesn't feel like hearing this. Three weeks later, it is astonishingly Henry's grandfather, who passed away some time ago, who appears physically and delivers the same message: "You will have thousands of souls to support."

Twice in three weeks. "It sounds pretty nice, why not?" Henry says to himself, but he doesn't picture himself starting right now. Why not when he's retired? Right now he's working in the world of fashion, which he is very passionate about.

Without paying attention to this request at the time, he continues in his professional life. He moves to Paris two years later, and just a few months after his arrival, a series of coincidences lead him to meet several mediums performing their work in public. One of them is named Mrs. Berthe. He does not know her, and yet during the public séance he attends, she looks at him and says, "I'm told you are a medium, your place is here with me." No! In Paris, Henry has found a job as a costume designer and is starting to make a name for himself in the world of show business. If he dreams of one thing, it's to be a singer. Intrigued, from time to time he continues to attend these group séances where mediums, sitting on a stage before a sparse audience, capture now and again any deceased people who are present and deliver their messages to their loved ones who are in the room.

It is in this setting that he gets to know the medium Nicole Leprince, with whom he will form a tight friendship. Their first encounter takes place during a private consultation in which Henry introduces himself as just a client. That day, his grandfather appears and gives him that same insistent message: "You will have thousands of souls to support . . ." This couldn't be happening! Despite his reluctance, something is set off in him, and in the months that follow (he has been in Paris less than a year), after having been tested by the organizer of the public séances, Henry finds himself on the stage.

His nerves that day are unimaginable, far stronger than what he might still experience today before beginning a public séance. The night before, unable to sleep, Henry drinks coffee after coffee and sleeps only three hours. And then the morning of that March 13, tormented by anxiety, he is on the brink of calling everything off. He wants to throw up. Still, as soon as he is up on stage, everything shifts, the anxiety has disappeared, and time has stopped. He is instantly inhabited by strange energies and picks up on the spirits as if he had done this all his life. Which actually is somewhat true.

A new and not unpleasing life is established. Henry participates in these public séances in the evenings, or on Saturdays, and continues his work as a costume designer. He is happy. It seems to him that he has followed the command that had seemed so imperious coming from his guide and his grandfather, all while continuing to do what he loves and what gives him satisfaction. But it seems that more is expected from him, and soon his guide intervenes again, this time in a very direct way: "Stop now or your gifts and aptitude will be taken from you." In other words, "Stop your career and become a medium full-time or else your capacity for perception will be taken away." This demand is final, and today he almost considers it as blackmail. He is being intimidated into helping parents in mourning, which he is already doing in public, feeling how useful he is in this task. But full-time? Receiving people in private? Despite his apprehension, everything happens very quickly. He abandons his career and the show business milieu he loves with a heavy heart. He is twenty-nine when he becomes a full-fledged medium. Today he is fifty-four.

So for years Henry has been consulting in this small apartment in southern Paris, plunged in darkness. After all of my visits, I have gotten to know him.

The photo of my father is now stuck to his forehead. After the intriguing start to the test, showing him the photo of my father had an instant effect on the channeling of information.

"I see papers," he tells me, "an iron box, I even hear noise inside the box. As if there were things inside the box, things belonging to him, many things. I sense someone who is relatively open but also conservative. He had a tendency not to want to see very many people, living a bit of a secluded life. He's making me feel these are the last years of his life . . . the world, family . . . 'in small doses,' he's saying, 'in small doses.'"

My father could not be better defined: a man enjoying living almost as a recluse. And this expression "in small doses" I can totally hear him saying over and over . . . Henry continues without me saying a word.

"'I wish people would just leave me alone!' he says to me. He was a little bit of a grouch now and then. He didn't talk a lot but I'm seeing him watching the world around him."

"Yes."

"He's saying to me: 'My wife had a lot of patience with me.' He's saying a sort of thank you for this. It's incredible, he's saying this sentence for the second time: 'I wish people would just leave me alone!' He's not talking about now, but when he was alive, the last years of his life. You see what I mean?"

"Yes. That makes sense to me. Actually, that makes a lot of sense."

"He's insisting, two more times even. Is there a window at his house with objects that belong to him?"

"Yes."

"It's in a room; some slightly old things are in this window, objects more tied to him than to the rest of the family. Objects to look at but not to touch."

"Yes."

This is amazing. Papa had installed shelves on the main wall in the living room where he had placed all kinds of objects from his childhood, things he had been given or inherited from his ancestors. He was extremely attached to them. He called it his "museum of objects."

"I'm seeing him surrounded by a beautiful light, and he's telling me, 'If I had known!' as if when he was alive he didn't really believe in the survival of the soul."

"Yes."

"He's showing an object you gave him. Like a cut mineral. I'm seeing it placed on his desk."

On his desk, Papa had placed a huge piece of petrified wood that I had brought him from Madagascar. A block that I had picked up today. But why, now that the connection seems to be established, doesn't my father say what I'm waiting for him to say and why is he talking about his museum of objects or the fossil on his desk instead?

I intervene: "Does he have other things to tell us?"

"Wait . . . this might seem strange, but he is sending me emotional thoughts toward someone from his youth. A nanny, or someone he considered to be his second mother? You don't know who it is?"

"I couldn't tell you."

At this stage in our interview, I really couldn't tell. My mother will nevertheless confirm several weeks later that during the Second World War, when Paris was occupied, my father was sent to the countryside by his parents to the home of a lady for whom he had a very great affection, and about whom he often spoke to my mother.

For the moment, Henry continues: "It's a lady he loved very much . . . Is there someone deceased in your family who was named Maurice? Or Mauricette?"

"I couldn't say."

"Maurice or Mauricette, a first name like that . . . He's letting me know that he liked things well done, that he was a perfectionist. Does that mean anything to you?"

"Yes."

He liked things well done, yes, but as far as Maurice or Mauricette, that was a mystery.

"He's telling me: 'When I was afraid I was wrong about something, I never let it show' . . . a question of pride. It's curious, I don't know who it is for you, or in his family, but is there one child who searched for a kind of recognition from him, does that make sense to you?"

"Yes."

"He's sending me this thought very strongly, the thought of a child who sought his approval, his recognition, his love. You understand?"

"Yes."

"It's very strong. I'm hearing, 'Now I understand.'"

My brothers and I always looked for our father's approval. Being the oldest one, I didn't suffer from his relative absence of demonstrations of affection as much as my two brothers did. They were much more affected by it. Before his death, Thomas had even been very clear about the hurt that he believed stemmed from not having received signs of love and attention from our father.

This information, about the lack of demonstrated affection our father showed toward us, will be given by all of the mediums participating in the test. This recurrence, just like the recurrence of his secluded and solitary nature, would be astonishing and a total surprise, statistically speaking, if—as certain people claim—mediums were describing character traits by chance, proving that they were the same each time *by coincidence*. These similarities concern not only my father's nature, as we will see throughout the book, but a number of other details as well, most notably when it comes to the circumstances of his death. Without revealing anything about what lies ahead, I must confess at this point that when, medium after medium, these precise constants begin to emerge, my incredulity will transform into real emotion.

But let's continue with Henry.

"This man didn't like getting shots?" he asks me, referring to my father in the photo.

"No."

"He's showing me the needles. He didn't like people giving him shots, or having people looking after him."

No one likes getting shots. But I can't help thinking back to my father suffering through ascites during the last months of his life, and about those long puncture appointments he had to endure, which consisted of sticking a needle into his stomach to draw out the excess gallons of fluid. Those appointments must certainly have brought relief, but they also must have been deeply unpleasant experiences.

"I'm repeating what I'm hearing, yeah? 'The doctor doesn't give a damn . . . no shots . . . no thingamajigs . . .'

He's got quite a personality, a lot of character in this man. I believe he was rather demanding but cheerful at the same time. I can see his little smile. I feel a great sensitivity . . . He must have had his rages at one time. I don't know if it was at the moment he departed from this world, or a little before, but he's appearing stiff with pain. His hands are squeezing someone or something, clenching. A sharp pain somewhere in the body."

"Yes."

My father could indeed lose his temper quickly, but he was also a kind man, always listening, and cheerful. As far as rages, he had them, that's for sure. And it was not a pretty sight.

"I feel like I'm being roughly grabbed by a searing pain and I'm tensing up. You understand?"

"Yes."

"My body is stiffening all at once as if I were going to leave. He's explaining that he died just after this pain, you see, does that make sense?"

"Yes."

"I feel this pain, he's showing me what it was like . . . It's funny because at the beginning he had me hearing about a kind of metal box that is opened, something that can be dug through, and now I'm hearing 'my boxes' or 'my box.' Does that mean something to you?"

"No."

The boxes don't bring anything in particular to mind. However, the pain he described was there, not necessarily intense and violent, but dull and grueling in his last weeks. I can see the mask that would sometimes appear on his face when he was seized by a sudden burst of pain, his hands squeezing . . .

"Is it him or his father who had a war medal?"

"His father."

"Because someone is up there with him, and has suddenly shown me a war medal, that's his dad?"

"That's his father, yes."

"Yes, they're together. Of course, this man, his father, left a long time ago. This man"—Henry points to the photo of my father—"admired his father, did you know that?"

A war medal, a son who admired his father . . . Of course, every dad old enough to be the father of the man in the photo could have been part of the wars that shook the world during the last century. Furthermore, it's also not much of a risk to say that a son admired his father. But I confirm to Henry to see if my targeted assistance will guide him.

"I think he admired him, yes."

"I sense that there was admiration, in a generation when those kinds of things were not said. Admiration for things he did during the war . . . The spirit who is deceased received war medals. Did someone hold onto those?"

"Uh . . . yes."

I don't know why I'm not reacting. I'm the one who salvaged my grandfather's *Croix de guerre*, the Cross of War. But the mention of a military medal probably seems still too vague at this point.

"It's one of the two . . . His father was wounded in the leg?"

"Yes."

"I have someone talking to me about a wound in the leg."

Now this is becoming clearer. My grandfather, who according to Henry has just stormed in next to my father showing his medal and talking about a wounded leg, had been decorated during the First World War, and also wounded in the feet and legs during the conflict. He had remained somewhat disabled for the rest of his life and endured almost daily suffering. My father, though, his only son, had indeed held great admiration for the man who died before I was born.

"He must have been rather cerebral, that man . . . Is it him or his father who had light eyes?"

My father had light blue eyes, but that doesn't show in the photo, and what's more we are still immersed in darkness.

"Him."

I answer as I point to the person in the photo, though, incidentally, Henry has strangely still not mentioned who he might represent for me. I obviously don't say anything, even if logic and a more precise examination could imply a certain family resemblance. This is actually the reason I didn't give great importance to the fact that mediums are able to identify him as my father. On the contrary, I am attached to the things that do not appear in the photo and that could not be deduced by examining it. The wound in my grandfather's leg in the First World War, for example, which of course could not be guessed at from a photo of his son.

"He had blue eyes?"

"Yes."

"I see blue eyes. I saw him looking at me eagerly . . . He's telling me that, when he was alive, he thought a great deal about his deceased loved ones. Without much conviction, he had hoped that survival after death was real. Does this mean something to you?"

"Yes."

The survival of the soul after death! Ever since my brother's death, his son's death, my father thought about it constantly, and oscillated between hope and resignation. He rarely opened up, but in the moments when just the two of us were talking, I would feel the suffering, the pain, and the sadness brought on by the doubt that consumed him every second. He seemed like a prisoner being tugged between contrary feelings. The books I had suggested he read didn't seem to significantly shake what he used to call, with sad panache, the "immense wall of fog." As a matter of fact, his tremendous erudition did not help him. Instead, it supplied him enough intellectual arguments to validate both hypotheses. What is there after death? Nothing or something? His heart was unable to make a decision.

"He's explaining that he didn't have a strong belief that life could continue after death. He wasn't sure. 'We'll certainly find out,' he thought. And he is sharing with me how astonished he was. He talks about a return to his roots. He's explaining that he gave little signs to certain people around him. Did you hear about that?"

"That sounds familiar."

My mother told me she had felt his presence. So had my brother Simon. And this had happened to me also. But in this kind of situation, things are so subtle and intimate that it's very delicate to objectively share what might have, for one person, been the force of something certain.

"He's explaining that he had to put some of his affairs in order."

"In what way?"

"Personal affairs . . . He must have had a room just for him at his house. Did you know that? Did he live in, at one time or near the end of his life, a place with a yard and a sort of shed, or an extension?"

"Yes, that was the case."

"He's explaining that it's a room separate from everything else, where he could stay for hours. Even passing the whole day there didn't bother him."

"Yes."

"He liked to be separate from everything in that room. He's talking to me about his occupations, his passions."

My father had taught geography to high school students, but he was a painter. Teaching had been his profession, and painting his essence. He had built a studio for himself some distance away from the house in the garden, where he spent the majority of his days: painting, of course, but also writing and reading. Even sitting in front of Henry, I can still feel in my entire being the *presence* of my father. I don't know how to explain it, but I feel it. At the same time, I am aware that this feeling is totally subjective, and that in order for this test to succeed, it should be impartial. I must manage to help Henry and my father concentrate on the objective, without directing things too much. I'm walking on eggshells.

"Can you ask him to describe his departure?"

"Yes, as long as he feels like talking about it," Henry responds. "His mother was a widow for a long time, I'd say twenty, twenty-five years?"

"Yes."

My grandmother died twenty years after her husband.

"Because he's telling me that his mom was a widow for many years. He's saying, 'I've found her, too.' She came to look for him, with her husband, they came together. He was happy to see them. 'I made peace with myself,' that's what I'm hearing; it's curious but I'm confiding this to you. If he says that, it's because he must have had somewhat of a tortured mind, he's making me feel it . . . Ouch, I don't want to say the wrong thing; I've just received a pain here, in my chest. Did he have a chest problem, heart or lungs?"

"Both."

"It was like an electric current that went through my chest and my heart in one blow."

After my brother's death in 2001, probably because of the colossal shock that had affected him so greatly, my father fell victim to a case of septicemia that led to his injuring a valve in his heart. He eventually was cured of the septicemia, but it had done some damage. After that episode, in fact, he started displaying cardiac fatigue caused by a very slight leak in the weakened valve. Over time, this fatigue had an effect on his lungs, weakening his body even more, until the moment that his heart gave out after weeks in the hospital and weeks of slow decline leading to his body's utter exhaustion. Ascites, that mass of water in his stomach, was a direct result of his pulmonary and cardiac problems. I am providing these details in the interest of allowing you to judge the accuracy of Henry's perceptions and those of all the mediums who participated in this book, which you will see later.

Back to Henry, and my father doesn't seem to want to dwell on seeing his body slowly letting him go, which he disliked.

"He's insisting on showing me that he had a kind of drawing in his house, no, a painting, representing something in nature, then the sun. Brightness, light . . ."

"Yes."

Hanging on the walls of my parents' house are numerous paintings done by my father, depicting everything, without exception: stylized landscapes seen from above, alternating with geometric shapes, lines, and sometimes large zones of color in the shape of a lake, a desert, a chain of mountains.

"He's showing me the room in the garden again, the one that's not in the house . . . where he spent a lot of time."

"Yes."

"He's showing me butterflies. He must have liked looking at the yard and the butterflies . . . observing them. I sense that it's the observation that matters most in the images he's showing me."

"Yes."

"Observing through a window in that little house. I see him very pensive. He's thinking about his life, the people around him, his family. A lot happened those last few years, he's telling me. As far as his family, I'm hearing, 'I'm still here.' He's whispering to me in a breath of air: 'I was scared.'"

My father adored his home. The idea of having to leave the sweet tranquility of his countryside, the singing of birds, the sweeping view over the crest of the forest, and the ballet of the kite birds was a huge heartbreak. Death meant leaving this paradise. During an exchange we had in the kitchen, as he was looking at the forest through the window, he suddenly asked me with great emotion in his voice, "Will there be landscapes like this after death? Will I be able to look out the window? Are there windows after death? It's not knowing that terrifies me." This was a few weeks before his passing, when the springtime and the sun were giving everything that was stretching out before his eyes the color of joy. He was touching on both the essence of life and, at the same time, what is so simple in it.

Making mediumship a career implies being paid for it. Even though many people practice a profession that they have a gift for to begin with, without the slightest objection being raised, the question is always up for debate when it comes to mediums. Why?

After all, doesn't a cook, for example, earn his living thanks to a gift he knew how to nurture? Like a musician, a florist, a painter, a writer, a lawyer, a surgeon or even a psychologist. Why should mediums, or healers for that matter, be the exception and work for free? Why would it be admirable to earn one's living (sometimes a very good one) by exploiting a gift for swimming, let's say, but reprehensible to do so as a medium?

"It's not the same," people retort. And why not? This pre-emptive assertion that healers or mediums should not put a price on a gift they have been given, lest they be called charla-tans, is it not related to the relationship our society maintains with unexplained abilities: a kind of fearful fascination mixed with suspicion?

Well, if so, then we must be aware just how much this attitude keeps us in ignorance of the reality of these phe-nomena. For what are these abilities, really? First of all, they are not nothing. These abilities exist, their reality has been observed—it is their interpretations that are still mysterious. But as for the ability of a man or a woman to obtain accu-rate information via a sort of sixth sense, the empirical ob-servation of results—in a laboratory setting, no less—should eliminate any doubt. Whether this information originates from a deceased person, or from telepathic abilities, or from something else entirely: *that* is a legitimate and even crucial question which this book attempts to answer.

Mediumship is a tangible and real phenomenon. It is not magic, nor is it sorcery or a power given by God or someone else. Research shows us that we are dealing with a natural tendency of the human being that is very developed in certain people, which demands to be tamed by the person in whom it awakens. Its use requires discernment on the part of both the medium and those who consult with them.

Being gifted does not make a medium a chosen one, no more than a very good baker is a chosen one. This gift, once developed and mastered, can be exploited professionally. Why on earth wouldn't this be possible? It is good practice for each individual to be judged in the same way that the Na-tional Council of the Medical Association does, by allowing the application of a code of ethics to be shared by all practi-tioners. But it would be illogical to judge an entire profession on the basis of presuppositions with no scientific foundation. It would not be responsible.

Not only do mediums and healers have the right to be paid, but denying them this would lead to the deviations we are trying to avoid. By not recognizing these abilities for what they are, we are giving credence to the fuzziness and ambiguity concerning the limits of their field, whether in healing or in the work of grieving. This is where the very real danger of sectarian offshoots, charlatanism, and scandalous abuses of all kinds lies.

So yes, like the others, Henry pondered this subject for a long time, and sometimes still does. To him, if there really were a spiritual conflict caused by his being paid, why would he have been asked to stop his other career? The command was so forceful! He would have preferred to remain a costume designer and occasionally help people during the public séances. Today, he does not regret changing his life, even if he misses his old one. Henry is a creative person. There is an artistic part of him deep within, and he has missed not being able to express it at several points in his life.

We have often had discussions on this subject, because I am struck by the steadfastness and the energy that Henry has, for more than twenty-five years, poured into doing the same thing: receiving the pain of people in mourning several times a day. I see this as a true calling that he takes on with an almost penitent sense of duty. He says he is helped and encouraged to continue this task because he feels useful in the midst of the distress and suffering of the people who come to see him, whether they are believers or skeptics, who are unanimously plunged into dismay by the loss of a loved one.

How many times has he been able to give people something that allowed them to imagine that the soul may continue living after death? In how many has he opened a small door toward hope? To how many people has he returned the strength to live when they no longer had any left?

I witnessed this several times. I have seen people light up and embrace him, like the policeman the week before our interview who had come to see him about his dead son. At the end of the séance, as he was leaving and standing on the doorstep, this man stopped in front of Henry and asked him suddenly if he could hug him. Which he did. At the mention of this recent episode, Henry is very moved. In these kinds of moments, I understand better why he has been in this strange career for so long.

I say strange because, far from being what most people believe, the life of a medium is not always rosy, and not necessarily one to be envied. Henry is not making a fortune, and he gave up a worthwhile career that was opening its arms to him. He lives amid the dead day and night; all this, in the end, for the smile of a mother, for the flash of hope he sees emerge in the eyes of a downcast father. No, this is not an easy job.

In addition, using his perceptions every day wears on him heavily on a physical level. Henry doesn't take care of his health. He is confronted daily with the psychic energy people are carrying, their emotions, but also those of spirits. Successfully tuning in, keeping up with the different stages as they develop, is enormously tiring. This has aged him. Henry matured very young. He became older than his age and grew up differently than other people in his generation.

Yet beyond all of these difficulties, he mentions joyful moments, remembering that extremely powerful things are also happening. Seeing his clients regain the strength to continue living is priceless. He confesses that providing proof of survival, giving faith back to those who had lost it, represents the greatest grace that he has been given in life.

It is hard to measure the weight of responsibility that the act of receiving people in mourning represents, especially without any formal training in psychology. Henry was at first very worried about this point in particular because he wanted to be able to give information about the deceased, to practice his mediumship, and also be able to psychologically support the people who were consulting him. Without training as a therapist, this is not accomplished by "playing the shrink," but by granting a blind confidence to the *invisible*. This confidence is needed when a person is meeting with people who tell you right from the start of the consultation: "Sir, if I don't have some kind of sign today, I'm going to kill myself." What responsibility! How can one imagine that this would be easy to go through? But most of all, how can one manage to calmly enter a state of perception? How does he do it? In his place I would be paralyzed by tremendous stress.

The key lies in his unwavering confidence in the invisible world, which allows him to bypass the emotional weight. Today, performing this activity for such a long time has helped him acquire certain automatic reflexes. "What's important is the letting go," he says.

First he has to be able to pull away from the person who has come for a consultation, along with that person's energy, expectations, and psychological and emotional state. During a private consultation, to attain this state of release, Henry closes his eyes. This is his way of isolating himself: not looking at the client. Once he is truly detached, he works on trying to ignore his own state of mind, which is the most difficult part. But when he begins concentrating, interfering thoughts emerge. So he prays, in silence, and makes himself available. Then, in this state of calm, he waits to be invaded. As if a sort of depersonalization were taking place. This is what he feels is happening: a part of himself depersonalizes and becomes the other person, the deceased. He lets himself be invaded by its psychic energy. It's a sort of balancing act because Henry remains completely conscious and in the present with the client across from him, all while being depersonalized. A part of him is invaded by the spirit universe soaking into him, and his task consists of saying out loud as much information as he can, repeating what the deceased communicates to him: images, sensations, feelings, and words that are their own.

At this point in the consultation, Henry can either feel the presence of the deceased in the room or even see them, behind or next to the client, for example. He can also receive internal images in which the spirit shows itself to him and leads him into a precise moment in its past.

Henry feels intentions that belong to the deceased. For example, during consultation, he transmits information that has been given to him, but sometimes the client doesn't react right away or doesn't understand. So Henry, who has noted that the spirit is passing onto something else, is surprised when the spirit suddenly returns to the subject that the client didn't understand to provide other details. Behind this spontaneity, Henry sees an intention, an insistence that has nothing to do with a static image or a memory belonging to the spirit.

This insistence on the part of the deceased really gives him the feeling that *someone* is communicating with him. He can feel their presence.

The beings that are speaking to him sometimes even cut him off when he is talking. This is far from being a minor detail; it's actually crucial. In fact, once it is apparent that the medium is capable of obtaining accurate information he didn't know before, the question of where he got this information presents itself. Henry thinks that a deceased person is transmitting it to him, but could it be a form of telepathy or seeing, as we posited earlier? Because from what we know today about extrasensory perceptions, the presence of a dead person is not necessary for obtaining information, however accurate, about a person that we don't know. Not to mention mentalism, which is an explainable technique.

There is nothing that can quantitatively allow us to choose objectively between the two hypotheses: that the dead are alive and talking, or that the medium is "only" a clairvoyant and telepathic. But there is this feeling, one that is certainly subjective but still essential. A clairvoyant perception doesn't cut somebody off; it doesn't force the medium to return to a detail they mentioned a little earlier. In a word, a clairvoyant perception does not show *intention*.

To explain this, Henry gives me a recent example of a mother who came to see him about her deceased daughter. All of a sudden, while he is talking with the mother, the young girl's spirit barges in through Henry, surprising him, and addresses her mother: "You see, Mom, I told you!" The young girl's presence was such that the fragile balance was forced apart and Henry fleetingly incorporated her for a few seconds. In a case like this, it is not enough to repeat what he is hearing, because the spirit is so impregnated in him that it is speaking directly from his mouth. Even though he sometimes has what we could call "fragments of incorporation," Henry does not like this feeling at all. It must be said that in the case of a total incorporation, the medium becomes completely unconscious, and does not remember anything afterwards. In Henry's case, he is conscious—it's just that he is no longer running anything for a few seconds. Sitting with that mother, it all came out at once: "You see, Mom? I told you!" The mother then told Henry that two days before her daughter's death, her daughter had announced that she was going to have a car accident and that she was going to die. Since the young girl was sixteen and couldn't drive, her mother had not paid that much attention to this remark. Well, it so happened that two days later, her daughter had been hit by a car while she was walking on the side of the road.

For Henry, such completely unexpected spontaneity is the proof, if there were still a need for any, that there truly is a living spirit, an intelligence that expresses itself through this contact with mediums.

Another time, two parents come to see him about their son who had died in a car crash. During the séance, the son shows a kind of postcard showing him in the mountains and tells Henry that he went to this landscape just before he died. The boy had died on the road in Brittany, so his parents respond to Henry, "No, sir, our son had not been in the mountains recently, he did not send us a postcard with mountains on it." But the son continues showing a card, as well as photos of him in the mountains. Henry tells the two parents that their son's spirit is insisting. They respond in turn: "No, it's been years since he's been in the mountains, this doesn't add up." So, despite the obstinacy on the other side—because the spirit had told him clearly that before dying he had been in the mountains—Henry apologizes and says he doesn't understand. A few days after the séance, the parents talk about their consultation with their loved ones, and their son's friend reveals to them that she and he had indeed gone and spent two days in the mountains before his death. They had even taken photos. When they came to the consultation, the parents knew nothing about this escapade, nor did Henry. In fact, only one person in the room was aware: their son, who had been dead for months.

The demands of clients can be lighter, less loaded. "How is so-and-so doing?" This is the most frequent request Henry receives from clients. He is also often asked if the dead have a particular message to give them. Many people come to see him out of curiosity. "Does life really exist after death?" This question is so dizzying! People also come to ask for advice from their deceased loved ones to help them make decisions in their life. In this case, Henry refuses. He believes that the spirits should not be disturbed for that kind of thing. His experience has led him to view his work as an opportunity offered to a spirit to come and prove his survival and to reassure the living. Sometimes, within this contact, the deceased may give information concerning the person who has come for the consultation, or their family, but that's different. Those deceased are coming spontaneously from their side.

I notice that what Henry is talking to me about, added to the way the test is playing out, suggests that rather than facilitating a communication, a discussion between two people, one dead and one living, via an intermediary, his abilities actually offer the dead the possibility of passing on brief messages. What they express spontaneously may be picked up by Henry, but asking them a question seems to be more complex. In fact, Henry confesses that he doesn't like being asked questions, for the very simple reason that he worries he will not have the answer. He is perfectly aware that he is the one blocked at this level. Nevertheless, his long practice has shown him that he often does receive answers from the dead to questions that the clients arrived with. The only difference is that he is not aware he is doing it, which makes a major difference, emotionally speaking.

This emotion, which seems to paralyze Henry, is certainly present as my test goes on in the small dark apartment.

I have the strange sensation of waking up from a dream. Deep down, I feel that my father is here. He is giving me facts that it would be difficult to attribute to chance, but he is not mentioning of his own accord what I'm expecting to hear from him. Why? I can palpably sense the annoyance Henry is feeling at not really knowing what I'm waiting for at the same time that he is certain that I am indeed waiting for something in particular. This fact is weighing on him, no matter what he says, and his unconscious, despite our friendship, cannot forget that I am testing him. He's putting pressure on himself, and I realize just how much this pressure is the enemy of his perceptions.

On the other hand, I feel that my father is present, but is it still my father? Who is this being speaking to me through Henry?

He is sometimes precise, describing his personality, his studio, his death, etc., but he jumps from one subject to another with a sort of inconsistency. Behind this character trait that doesn't seem like him, I notice his intention to try, via all of these details, to find one that will be convincing and striking enough to convince me once and for all that he is here. I can sense him almost feverishly trying to make himself understood by a medium who is slightly tense himself. But why doesn't he just tell me himself what I'm waiting to hear?

I decide at that point to help Henry hone in on the goal. So, pointing to the person in the photo, I become more precise.

"I asked him to pass something along."

"To who? The family?"

"To us, to you. For this book, I asked him to express something through each of the mediums I meet. A message . . . He knows what he has to say."

"A message for the book?"

"Yes. Before coming, I spoke to him and asked him to tell you something specific."

"But that's not so easy, Stéphane."

"No, not so easy at all."

"When everything comes spontaneously from their end, okay, but asking is no simple thing. At least not for me."

"Are there images coming to you?"

"No, not in relation to what you're asking me. But it's strange, he's telling me that he thought his coffin was too small. He's showing it to me, I don't know why, this is a little weird . . . I have this feeling that it's not wide enough, is it supposed to imply that he was a prisoner of something? No, he's not trapped inside matter, relax, you don't have to worry about him. I don't know . . . Is it related to the way he lived? His imagination? Do you understand?"

I observe that without saying anything to lead him in that direction, the mention of a specific message from my father leads Henry to talk about his casket. Mere coincidence?

"What I asked him to tell you is related to his casket."

"Ah, so this interests me . . . okay."

"Don't hesitate to share all of the sensations."

"He's talking to me about the casket and telling me that it's too small, that he has to push to be free . . . I heard your question, and he's talking to me about that."

"Even if you think it has nothing to do with anything and seems strange to you, say everything that comes to you."

"Yes . . . he's showing me . . . Everything is white, there must have been a fabric, white satin in the casket."

"Yes."

"The white color of the white satin. Okay, I'll say what I'm hearing: 'They put me in well.' He's saying thank you because I'm hearing, 'Thank you.' At the same time I understand that he liked simple things, that he wanted simple things, do you understand this?"

"Yes."

"Without flourishes, simple, he's insisting on this . . . I'm sensing a little bit of irritation. What I'm going to tell you is a little stupid but he's showing me an apple, I don't know why. A circular apple, I can't see very well what the meaning behind it is . . . I don't know. He's insisting, and at the same time it's not an easy thing, it's far from all this, but he's showing me his fingers, his fingers, his hand . . ."

And if Papa, not knowing how to communicate through Henry, were trying several things, insisting, and almost irritated? How else would he say things? When he shows his fingers, his hands, is he trying to talk about painting? And the apple? Why did Henry specify that it is a "circular apple"? Are there any that are square? Is this a symbol?

"I'm not seeing the object, but I can't stop seeing the finger, the hand, the finger, the hand . . . He's saying, 'I'm saying thank you . . . freedom, freedom . . . I am free.' Someone must have written a very beautiful text meant for him; it touched him very much, do you know what it is?"

Is the "very beautiful text" not *The Tartar Steppe*, which had moved him so much, the story of a man who remains until the twilight of his life the prisoner of a destiny that was forced upon him? In the moment, thinking more of the funeral service during which several beautiful things were said, I respond: "Yes, that is true."

"Could we say that there is something in his casket, or that things were put inside by his loved ones?"

Ah, now we're getting there! My help consisted of telling Henry that the man in the photo had a message to give me. Henry had then mentioned the casket being too small, then, dead on, the objects put into the casket by his loved ones. The message is really and truly a list of objects placed by a loved one into the casket! Could it also be a logical deduction from the fact that I said the message had to do with the casket? That's also possible.

For the moment, I say yes to Henry's question.

"Things, personal objects, from people who love him, and who put them in with him?" he asks.

I note that my father has moved Henry on to the idea that there are several objects and not just one. His efforts are almost palpable, even if a part of me still has a hard time understanding why he isn't simply saying what they are.

I ask: "Could he describe these things for me?"

"Personal things were put with him, I think it's more than one. When I say that, are we on the same page?"

"That there are several objects?"

"Yes, or several things; you don't know?"

"Yes, I know."

"He's having me feel several things."

"Tell me everything that comes into your head."

"I'm doing that, because he's sending me things, but at the same time he's detached from all this. He's happy, and he's thanking you: 'I will never be dead as long I'm alive here and here.'"

Henry points to my head and my heart. Why this sudden and so intimate remark? Henry never mentioned our bond.

"To the people who love him, friends and family, I'm hearing his voice in a whisper, very far away: 'Peace.'"

I didn't hear because Henry had murmured, and I make him repeat it.

"'Peace.' By this he means he is at peace . . . He has several objects with him . . . I'm trying to understand. Can we say there is something that has traveled, that was overseas?"

I hold back any untimely show of emotion, but the expression "something that has traveled" makes me instantly think about the compass. Once again, I put myself in my father's place, and I imagine him having to evoke these objects without using words. Yes, there you have it, that's probably it: he cannot say words but can only share sensations with Henry. Their zone of dialogue and communication is not located in a world of words but in a world of images and feelings. And what is the *feeling* of a compass?

I allow myself just, "Yes."

"I don't know what it is. Something that has traveled overseas, that someone put with him."

"That makes sense."

"He's insisting strongly on this: 'It's with me.' Yes, I heard, but I didn't see what it is . . . it's like an intention of the heart, a gesture . . . With his hand, he's picking up dirt, or sand; he's letting it escape . . . you see, as if everything were turning into powder."

"Sand?"

"Yes, what he's holding in his hand is like sand and he's going like this . . . You don't know what it is?"

Now I feel a shock; I'm very shaken but I don't show anything. Such true emotion because I have the feeling that my father is really trying very hard. Even I couldn't have thought of that. I realize once again how difficult it might be to give the title of the novel I placed in his casket. And to think that on the way to our meeting this morning I had spoken to my father aloud to ask him to try to mention the book out of all four objects! What synchronicity between my act of thinking specifically about the difficulty Papa would have in naming the book for me, and the fact that it is precisely this difficult point that *comes out* during the séance! *The Tartar Steppe*: what could better suggest the desert steppe than to take a fistful of sand and let it escape from his hand . . . a movement that Henry is reproducing before my eyes?

Despite my turmoil, I allow myself to say, "Yes, that's quite telling."

"Oh really, that's telling for you?"

"Yes."

"He's doing this with his hand in the shape of a cup, he's letting go of something that falls into his hand, a little like sand. This is what I see, what he's showing me, but beyond that I can't do more, Stéphane."

"All right."

"Now I'm getting tired. I can't go further."

"Let's stop. But I would like to understand why he can't give you just one word."

"Sometimes that's the case, sometimes it's not."

"Because I can really see that you're picking up on him, I feel like he is just on the other side, trying to communicate, and he knows what I'm waiting for. So he's giving images that speak for themselves, but why isn't he giving any words? Is he unable to do it or is it you?"

"It depends on the moment, on the spirit, it depends on so many factors . . . but the sand in the hand means something to you?"

"Yes."

"Because he tried to answer you. So you got a part of the answer and another part is missing?"

"But why did he use an image rather than a word? I can't tell you anything else, but I'm really wondering . . . I feel like we're beating around the bush."

"He did what he could."

"Why isn't he able to speak, or to say a certain word if you can hear him?"

"He *is* able to, but in bits and pieces. He's trying."

"But I'm expecting specific information and he knows this."

"And sometimes he's giving other information."

"Yes. But I still think that if he were alive next to us, phys-ically, I mean, still in his body, he would know exactly what to say and how to say it. So why is this different, since you're saying he is here? Why is he not saying clearly what he knows I'm waiting for?"

"I don't know. He started having me feel things, but what happened then? I'm talking about my perception. Was I blocked? Or did I block myself, and while he tried to put me on the right path, I unconsciously confused myself and without realizing it I'm not able to go further? It may also be that this is coming from the psychic energy field of your expectation. The result being that my end is blocked and he is not able to go any further."

"You mean he might also be having a hard time saying the words I'm expecting?"

"That could be, yes; obviously there are lots of different scenarios."

"This is what I would like to understand: what are the different scenarios you're mentioning? Is he not in good health where he is? Does he not know where he is?"

"No, that's not the case for him. He tried making an effort, but then again, in communication with the beyond there are what we call 'filters.' The psychic energies of the living and the spirit become mixed together during the process of perception. Sometimes I can't manage to bring myself up to speed with it in order to have answers to all the questions people would like to ask. Like you today, when something is blocked. This may not come from the deceased but from me, because, for example, I sense that you have a very strong expectation and that paralyzes me. In other cases, it could be the deceased who are not entirely open. Or else certain deceased people don't work well with certain mediums. It might be a question of empathy, energy. As if a part of their vibration were missing. It's a bit like us in our human encounters: sometimes there's a connection between two people, sometimes there isn't. And sometimes I'm tired and for some strange reason I do a magnificent séance. The deceased speak to me with their words, their expressions. I'm sometimes inside an unbelievable energy and density. I pick up on behaviors, body language, and the clients will confirm things by telling me, 'That's just like him!' or 'It feels like we're with him!'"

Was the test successful with Henry? I will let you be the judge; as far as I'm concerned, my heart has given me the answer. But what should we take away from this first meeting? Here, again, it is not for me to decide on your behalf, but I am very happy that I didn't back down and that I pushed my friend Henry to his limits. In the meetings that will follow, I will come across astonishing discoveries, and each time, just like today, I will do so with great emotion.

I can admit this to you: I really feel that my father was there throughout the meeting. I could feel him struggling sometimes, but he also amused me with his tenacity. I am creating this book with the mediums . . . and with him.

This is proof for me.

But hold on, when he's not having fun with his son, what is my father doing now that he has crossed over the immense wall of fog?

After probably thousands of consultations, Henry retains an amazingly limited vision of the beyond. The reason for this, according to him, is that he is not accessing the *location* where the deceased are. They are the ones who come to him. More precisely, they meet him halfway: they descend toward the physical, and he rises to another level of consciousness. During his contact with them, Henry explains that the deceased have lowered their rate of vibration in order to reach our reality. He doesn't think he can make it onto their level, but that they can descend by slowing down their vibrations. By doing this, they are synchronizing themselves, in a way, with the level we are moving around in. What he can gather about their dimension is that it is more ethereal than ours.

During medium contact, he is aware of being in a kind of light-filled space. He says he quite likes the moments when he sees the deceased appear, surrounded by a radiating luminous field. The vision of this conflagration immediately indicates to him what stage they are at. At times he can see only a neat outline of light, and at others it is translucent faces that appear. When Henry finds himself with deceased people who are showing up in their bodies, he sees their radiance. It is striking, he says with emotion. When this happens, he confesses that he no longer has the desire to return to our reality.

To this I add the fact that—and this is often mentioned among various traditions and by mediums—the dead can find themselves at different levels once they are on the other side. Access to one level or another would correspond to the deceased's understanding of their state and the way, rapidly or not, that they became aware of their death. This process may be more or less cumbersome depending on the person. Certain souls feel uncomfortable; they can only be partially aware of what is happening and cannot manage to free themselves from this confusion.

When the deceased are not aware of being dead, in general Henry does not pick up on them. They are said to be in a kind of reparative sleep. It is actually recommended to wait a little bit after a death before going to see a medium. Henry advises a minimum of three months (the dead can communicate earlier than that, but three months is an average). This time of reparative sleep corresponds to a necessary period after death during which the deceased person can free themselves from the mental body. "This famous mind that sometimes complicates our life here, why would it disappear in the blink of an eye?" Henry says. Our thoughts and our regrets continue to play in a loop. It takes time to see things more clearly. A person can be aware of being dead, completely aware, and yet not see the spirits who are coming to look for them. Henry has seen deceased people who are unaware, not sensing that they are surrounded by loved ones on the other side. He remembers a noteworthy experience similar to this. One day he entered into contact with a spirit who had died only a few months before. Filled with the spirit's energy, he perceived what he saw as small sequences. But they were going by at an indescribable speed, and soon Henry realized that this man was actually seeing the film of his existence, over and over, without being able to pull himself out of it. It was going in all directions, and everything was going too fast.

The deceased can also be aware of having died, but be constrained by the details of their life on earth that have not yet been resolved. A person can be aware that they have passed to the other side, but still have to accept their wrongdoings and forgive the living.

Then there are those who cannot accept their passing, or those who are not totally liberated because they feel the need for help that the living are experiencing. So they stay to support them, repair something, etc. The deceased may actually be perfectly unconstrained, but the needs of those who are still living creates an energy that holds them back in a less elevated plane, even though they are ready to move on toward another spiritual level. In a way, they hold themselves back for us. Henry insists on this point, in fact, and he is often a witness to the sometimes deadly weight of emotional ties that are so significant that pain prevents the living from moving on. For Henry, as for all of the other mediums I consulted, people must be able to allow the dead to follow their path. They repeat this often to their clients: our dead loved ones must move forward on their side. Death does not mean that they have abandoned us. We have to try to put ourselves in their place and imagine that not wanting to move beyond our own suffering could make them feel guilty. By doing this we are drawing them constantly back to us.

In these kinds of situations, imagine them as powerless witnesses to our pain. How do you think the people we have lost would like us to live? They are alive. Everything has not stopped with their departure, everything is not frozen in suffering, even if this may seem to be the case because of the absence created by a death in the lives of the people who stay behind, us. We must think of them as beings who are continuing their life.

Henry demonstrates consistency here by asking people not to abuse their consultations with mediums. He observes the same thing that many psychologists do: we are in the world of the living, and the suffering caused by a loss is eased when we engage in a process of mourning, which includes learning how to live with the absence and developing other relationships.[5]

When we have had the good fortune to receive, either from a medium or from ourselves, a truly convincing demonstration, we must be able to appreciate how exceptional it is. "And say thank you," Henry says. "If we request contact all the time, this could be paralyzing for the spirit because it is no longer in a position to follow its own path. We will never forget that we are always linked to them, even if we are not in contact with them."

---

5   On this subject, see the interview with Dr. Christophe Fauré on page 219.

Dominique

I am meeting medium Dominique Vallée at her home in a large Paris suburb. The sun is flooding the small yard that is accessed through a modestly sized veranda. This very bright room is where Dominique usually has her consultations. But we decide to go inside, and her dog, who has been celebrating my arrival from the moment I walked in, follows, bouncing alongside us.

Dominique has laughing, twinkling eyes. I have known her for several years, and have seen how seriously she takes her role in this quite distinctive activity. She agreed wholeheartedly to participate in this test, but I sense that she is terribly anxious. I'm worried this might affect the quality of the experiment. I have also decided to begin the séance with the photo right away. In the grand scheme of things this won't change anything—I'm giving her a photo she's never seen, and she doesn't know who the individual in the picture is—but this will allow her to concentrate on one person from the start, rather than reacting to all of the potential spirits that might be accompanying me.

As we take our places at the table, Dominique tells me what she always tells every person who comes to see her.

To begin, she explains that being a medium does not mean she has a magic wand. Even if a medium is successful 99 percent of the time, he or she may often encounter a failure. There are multiple reasons for this. For example, the deceased that a person is trying to contact may have had a difficult departure, or one that was too fast, and they may be in a zone of turbulence where they will be trying harder to get closer to the earth instead of rising above it. When the deceased find themselves in this zone, paradoxically, Dominique cannot connect with them. This makes me think of what Henry Vignaud says about the necessity of letting a certain amount of time go by between the moment of death and the first meeting with a medium, so that the deceased can detach themselves properly. Dominique has observed that communication depends on the position of the soul she is contacting.

Second, she recommends that clients record the séance, and if they don't do that, that they at least write down what is said so that information is not lost. For if, in the moment, certain details don't bring anything to mind, they may prove to be crucial a few days later with some emotional distance.

Finally, Dominique is very clear about the way the séance must begin: while the deceased person is trying to identify themselves, she does not want to know a single detail or hear a single question. The less she knows, the more effective she is. Also, in this first phase, she asks clients to only respond with yes or no to the specific questions she asks, without providing any additional explanations. At this stage, she just needs these markers to know whether or not she is in contact with the right deceased individual.

Evidently—I keep realizing this again and again—the need for identification reveals something rather significant: there are a ton of people up there. Perhaps it would be better to say that there are a ton of people *around us*. When the medium puts themselves psychically in a place of reception and opens their perception doors, they are lit up by a powerful projector in a parallel world, the world of the dead; they become visible to many of the deceased and, attracted by this living person who seems to see and hear them, many of the disappeared come close to the medium, impatient to be able to communicate.

(When you practice spiritualism for fun, exactly the same thing happens; you're putting a spotlight on yourself and becoming visible in the world of the dead. In general, those who wander that world on the lookout for a little light are not those you would want to invite to dinner. But once you've said hello to them, they know how to find the warm and welcoming house. So here's a tip: don't play around with that. It's not a game.)

All mediums protect themselves, and know how to do it. In fact, at the end of our interview, Henry confides to me that for a long time he had been invaded against his will. Everyone I talk to reminds people how careful they must be, because there are two forces present: the negative and the positive. In this way, the spiritual plane is not really so different from our material world, where light stands alongside the most sordid of shadows. Each world is a reflection of the other one.

The photo is placed flat on the table. Dominique wanted to give me the preamble without looking at it, then her eyes lowered to my father, her fingers brushed the image, and instantly things have started.

"Oh dear, there's a heart problem . . . He's having trouble breathing."

Dominique's reaction is very sudden, even physical, as if her own body is a soundboard for what she perceives.

I ask her, "What are you feeling?"

"Oh my goodness! I've had him for a while, this man. There is actually a kind of resemblance. This is your dad?"

"Yes."

Dominique tells me honestly that this information is a deduction and not a perception. But as I explained to her previously, I am not including this recognition as part of the test.

"Seeing the photo has really heightened my emotions. I'm feeling him having a lot of respiratory difficulty. When I was speaking to you at the beginning, I was already working with him because I was having trouble breathing. Did he have this kind of problem?"

"Yes."

"Your dad is someone who's a little torn in two; he can be pretty tough and at the same time he's someone with a sense of humor. He's also a very sensitive person . . . There's a lot of emotion; he almost made me cry, actually."

"A very sensitive person." My father projected the image of a man living inside his bubble. But in the rare moments when he allowed himself to come a little bit out of that shell and express his emotions, they overwhelmed him. Many years ago, when I was a young journalist who never stopped asking him for writing advice, he had snatched up from his desk a volume of Nicolas Gogol's work published by La Pléiade and began reading me a passage aloud from "The Overcoat" so that I could hear the musicality. We had gone out onto the terrace in front of his studio, but after a few sentences his tears had quickly forced him to stop, overwhelmed by what he was reading. That was a lesson I never forgot. A few well-written sentences, restrained and true, from this great Russian writer had hatched the distress of the character in the story, Akaki Akakievitch, in my father's heart. Russian writers are great authors, certainly, but my father can still be classified as a "sensitive man." An emotional person beneath a thick steel shell.

But shells, as thick as they are, only protect us from what's outside. Never from what is seething inside of us.

"Okay, I know the story of Thomas, and I know that interferes," Dominique continues, "but one thing's for sure: he never got over it. He's telling me that he never got over it . . . There is also perhaps a certain amount of guilt on his part. Not about the accident itself but guilt as a father, in relation to Thomas's personality, you see?"

"Yes."

Dominique knows the story of my brother Thomas's death, just like nearly all of the mediums I will see. However, this event probably has greater significance for her because she lost her own son the same year I lost my brother. And her son was also named Thomas. I still make a mental note that there is one thing she doesn't know, which Henry also picked up on: the relationship between my brother and my father. She will return to this later.

"He's very proud of his children, of what you all have become. Your father is interested in many subjects. There are lots of things around him, paintings, sculptures; he's passionate about this."

My father was a painter and my mother a sculptor. Dominique seems to be capturing many small details at the same time that she is experiencing the sensations and feelings that belonged to my father's life. As if her mediumship were corporal. It's very pronounced.

"His health problem was a long one . . . He departed not very long ago, is that right?"

"Yes."

"Did his respiratory problem last a long time? Answer me with just yes or no."

"Yes."

"I get the feeling that there's something encumbering him

. . . I'm getting the idea of suffocation . . . He's also someone who can be very warmhearted. I see him: he's taking people in his arms, patting them on the back."

My father's heart problem had affected his lungs very early on, and the last months of his life were difficult on the respiratory level. I have been noticing another curious thing since the beginning of the séance: each time that Dominique mentions a period of illness, my father leads her toward more pleasant feelings. Why?

"He's talking to me about Coco; he has a parrot? What is Coco? Or Cloclo?"

My mother's name is Claude. My father didn't call her Cloclo but he would sometimes use the nickname to tease her. This séance is really starting to get interesting. I answer Dominique: "It might have to do with Claude, my mother."

Is mediumship an ability inherited from one's ancestors? Dominique Vallée's grandmother was what we would call a "sleeper." A sort of healer or seer, or both, that people would consult at a time when medicine was not as accessible as it is today and when going to the doctor was expensive. People would come to see this good woman carrying the clothing of the sick person. She would then fall into a narcoleptic episode—that's where the term "sleeper" comes from—and during this time of strange sleepiness, she would magnetize the piece of clothing, announcing her diagnosis and giving instructions. Even if this term and this practice are forgotten today, it is clear that her granddaughter developed the same aptitude for care and subtle perception at a very early age. But curiously, no one spoke about this grandmother who departed before her birth, and it was not until much later that Dominique would discover that she possessed these gifts.

Still, when she is a child, her father—who had been in a very serious accident and still experienced pain as a result—often asks her to put her hands on his head. *What is he making me do? This is stupid*, the young girl thinks. But following her dad's request, she runs to wash her hands and does it without really understanding a whole lot. One day she overhears a small mysterious sentence in the course of a conversation between her father and mother: "Dominique is like Maman." Her father understands perfectly that she has inherited her grandmother's abilities, but this is the only time he will speak of it. He will never broach the subject with her, as if he wants to hide this information from her until the end of his days.

As an adult, Dominique understands why her father never encouraged her gift: being a magnetizer is not a career. Since that time, after spending part of her childhood in the countryside where, as a solitary little girl, she took care of sick or wounded animals without knowing why, her existence seems to be sailing toward a more traditional horizon. But don't we always say that a person's life path eventually catches up with them?

Now a teenager, her baccalaureate in the bag, Dominique gets a degree in history and geography. But she realizes that teaching hardly tempts her, so she takes a sabbatical year and works at the Society for the Protection of Animals (SPA). Overwhelmed by her discovery of the woes of mistreated animals, she turns toward a veterinary assistant's certification. It is then that her genes are finally expressed: she becomes involved in caring for others.

During the years in which she is progressively becoming more herself, love arrives. She meets a man and soon gives birth to a child. Her husband is a manufacturer and works in construction. He is light-years away from magnetism, but he respects his wife's choices and does not prevent her from continuing her occasional work as a healer. In reality, it's not so much that he doesn't believe in it, but he is a little afraid of it. Not of the healing, but of Dominique's perceptions, her sharpening senses that touch the taboo subject of death. How many of us would prefer to leave those doors closed? To never talk about it? To think about it as late as possible, as if it were never really going to happen?

Denial is human. And more often than not, we prefer not to look what bothers us in the face, even if it is inescapable.

The husband works, and Dominique opens herself to the invisible, but the couple never discusses the subject. As for Dominique's in-laws—several of whom are graduates of polytechnic school—they see her practice as a magnetizer as something rather strange. "I think if I had been working the streets, it would have been the same, they didn't understand." So in that case, really, it's better not to say anything. This is what she does for years.

For a thousand different reasons, the relationship between the couple is not working, and one day Dominique leaves this life and this man. Shortly after, she decides to throw herself completely into caring for others, and opens her practice in Saint-Germain-en-Laye. She is twenty-five.

The call is too strong. Until now, she received people in her home, but the need for an office has slowly sprouted. Why begin working full-time in a career that scares people? A rather delicate profession that she can't talk about very much? Because Dominique simply doesn't have a choice. When she is caring for someone else, when she is able to ease another person's discomfort, she feels so good doing it. She is in her place.

Around this time, Dominique crosses paths with an oncologist at a riding stable she goes to often. She adores horses, and indeed still takes care of them today. When the physician discovers she is a magnetizer, he regards her with suspicion. Then they get to know each other, and one day the man asks Dominique if she would be able to remove a wart for him. It's in her blood. The wart disappears. A warm friendship develops between them. During a conversation some time later, Dominique notices the oncologist's deceased grandfather standing next to his grandson. She doesn't know why, but she opens herself up to him, and the information she delivers to the doctor completely shocks him.

But it also shocks Dominique.

In fact, these perceptions of the deceased during magnetism séances are becoming more and more frequent. From that point on, Dominique regularly observes that when she is caring for someone, she also receives details, images, and flashes. Sometimes the deceased even introduce themselves to her. It's embarrassing. How is she supposed to react? What should she do? What should she say? How is she supposed to tell this lady who has come to her about shingles, for example, that standing behind her is a man with a beautiful English mustache, a Hawaiian shirt, and a tan? She says something, and the lady responds, completely overwhelmed: "But that's my husband, he died twenty-five years ago."

Is it because every time Dominique notices the presence of the deceased she finds the right words? Without fail, the people she feels she can talk to about her perceptions and to whom she can deliver messages from dead loved ones react quite positively, and are even grateful to her for this unexpected help. Particularly the young woman around whom Dominique sees a man dressed in an undershirt. Her perception is quite striking because it is rather dense: a man with an undershirt in sweltering heat. Confident in the sharpness of her sensation, she describes her vision to the young girl, and asks if she knows what it's about. "No, not at all!" Yet the man is presenting himself as her father. Dominique tells her this. Then the young girl realizes: "Yes, my father, that's right! He worked in a foundry. Now I understand better why there's the undershirt and the extreme heat." So Dominique gives her the message she is receiving: this man has things he is ashamed of, he needs to ask for forgiveness. At these words, the young girl suddenly starts sobbing. She soon reveals to Dominique that she had been subjected to sexual violence by her father, with the tacit consent of her mother, who had never done anything about it. This spontaneous and completely unplanned séance as a medium would mark the beginning of the liberation of this young woman, who until then was having a disastrous emotional life and carrying all of that accumulated suffering inside of her, the detrimental weight of what is unsaid.

Experiences like this one also reinforce Dominique's confidence in her perceptions. She feels she is legitimate, and the messages she is transmitting are useful. So much so that one day—more than twenty-five years ago—she decides to stop her care practice and work exclusively as a medium. At the time she does not plan to practice both activities, magnetizer and medium, at the same time. In her eyes this would make her seem less credible. In hindsight she believes she made a huge error, for this decision was more motivated by the fear of being badly perceived by other people than whether she felt capable of doing it.

Her work as a medium is falling gently into place, even though at this time she has to fight against some heavy prejudice. But wasn't that probably to be expected, too? Has she always been a medium? A childhood memory seems to attest to this. When she was quite little, Dominique had a very strange experience several times with a photo of her grandmother, the famous sleeper she had never known. The photo of the old woman was in a frame hanging on the wall in her parents' house. Dominique remembers distinctly the somewhat strange moments when the woman in the photo would come down out of the frame, give Dominique a kiss, then go back up into her frame. An early medium perception? Dominique spoke about it once to her father. It seemed as though the world had opened up under his feet. He had wanted his daughter to become a lawyer or a teacher! But no, the grandmother's gift was definitively in the little girl's genes.

The séance continues as Dominique obtains more and more precise details about my mother from my father, her husband. I need to insert a clarification here to dispel any ambiguity. I know that the information about my father being a painter and my mother being a sculptor is accessible to everyone, either online or in my writings. But that's it. Many of the other details that the medium has given me up to this point are impossible to find anywhere. Unless one is a member of my close family, which is not the case for these mediums.

I remain very attentive both to what is said and to the order in which the information emerges, as well as the way it is stated. I have been able to observe that when the mediums consulted in the context of this book were aware of one biographical detail or another concerning me, they did not make a secret of it, just as Dominique was very clear about her knowledge of my research after Thomas's death and my writings. She did not try to disguise what she knew already as one of her perceptions. This would have been vulgar, and obviously cheating. I should add that the tests conducted for this book were done in an atmosphere of mutual trust. When it came to my methods I was sometimes very tough and often extremely demanding. But this does not impede trust. And I have great trust in the people I met during those long months of inquiry, just as they have trust in my integrity.

Also, let's be clear: when Dominique says she is learning something from my father, I know that she is not play acting, just like all of the other mediums in this book. But to preserve this test's indisputable objectivity, I am proposing that you only give credence to the information regarding my father's personality, the details about the end of his life, his illness, and his passions. This information is not known outside of a very tight family circle. Finally, don't forget that when I go to each of the mediums, they are not aware of who my "target" is. They do not know who is in the photo I am going to give them. They don't know that I am going to be focusing on my father. And one last detail: there's the test, the objects I placed in the casket. Well, there is only one living person and one deceased person in the world who know about them: me and my father. And Dominique has a heck of a surprise in store for me on this subject.

Back to the séance, and my mother.

"Does this woman have a problem with her thumbs, her hands?"

"I don't know."

"As if she had worked a lot with her hands. She's kneading, I don't know if it's dough."

My mother, as I said, is a sculptor. She has never really mentioned anything to me about pain in her hands, but she has worked a great deal with the earth. She has sculpted stone and wood, but also made tremendous amounts of pottery, and today she no longer works with anything but the earth.

"Is your dad someone who traveled a lot?"

"Yes."

"Because I'm seeing the trip, he's a bit of an adventurer. He didn't have a very easy childhood, did he? Did he feel abandoned at one time in his childhood?"

"I don't know."

"Abandoned either due to the absence of his father, or his mother, or the fact that he had been put in boarding school very young."

"I don't know," I say, but it's pretty interesting that he's giving me information I wasn't aware of but that I could verify later on.

Which is the case. I know that my father was an only child, but while we are discussing this séance weeks later, my mother tells me that she had gotten the sense that during my father's childhood, his own father must not have been very present. Not to mention the war breaking out, then the Occupation, when my father, a young teenager at the time, left to live by himself in the countryside. This difficult childhood is incidentally something that several other mediums mention.

"He's a very reserved person, your dad, anything that touches something private, he has a hard time. He came to me very quickly, but there are things he didn't talk about on earth, and on the other side he still has a little trouble talking about them, it's who he is . . . It's almost like your mom's family was more his family than his own relatives."

This is something astonishing, yet another thing I don't know that my mother will reveal to me later. About his wife's parents, my father used to say, "I have finally found my family." Not that he didn't love his own parents, but he had discovered a large family, one that was perhaps more jovial, easygoing. Dominique continues.

"It's like he had been adopted by your mom's family, who may have been more warm, more laid-back, nicer."

It's peculiar—Dominique talks to me with visible ease,

then her gaze goes back into the void for a few seconds, she listens attentively and simultaneously transmits what she's channeling, without this back-and-forth seeming to bother her. And she always has these physical manifestations that make her start breathing exactly the same way my father did, searching for air with a large inhale. She punctuates the conversation by saying, "He's sighing." I feel like I'm seeing him this very moment; it's startling.

"Is he giving classes? There are a lot of people around him, young people, and he's sharing his knowledge."

"Yes, he was a teacher."

"Ah, he was a teacher? Why is there also art, painting, and sculpture?"

"He was a painter, it was his passion. His career was teaching."

Now I really can't believe how accurate Dominique is being. But it's not over yet.

"Were his trips connected to his teaching? Because he's bringing me over different countries."

"Yes, he taught geography."

"Still, he was at the end of his rope, he had a sadness in him. He tried not to show it for your mom's sake, but this departure is a real break."

"This departure?"

"Thomas's. He doesn't understand his personality, he's telling me again. He probably could have listened to him more, or been a little less hard on him. I think there is something he didn't understand or that he maybe hadn't imagined happening."

As I said earlier, Thomas suffered as a result of the distance he felt between him and our father, to the point of loudly making this known to him on several occasions. It's astonishing to see this detail emerge again.

"Does he want to talk about it?"

"They must have talked about it up there. Now it's as if they were able to touch one another . . . I don't know if it's something they did very often because Thomas was a highly sensitive person . . . Who is Pierre, or Jean-Pierre?"

"That's my father's first name: Jean-Pierre."

This avalanche of details is pretty staggering. It's not so much my father's name that overwhelms me most, but these details about his relationship with my brother Thomas, his personality, his capacity to feel emotion.

"You know, with the mention of Thomas we're moving too close to emotions for him. All of this sorrow he's making me feel . . . as a mom who has experienced similar things myself, he trusts me. I finally feel he's really being nice to me. Like he's saying to me: 'Okay, stop, this is hurting everyone, that's enough, and up here we were able to find each other again.' It's funny, regarding Thomas I'm now getting an image of freedom. Your brother, as if he were with my son. Mine was an Alpine hunter, he was someone who did a lot of skiing, climbing, he was very physical. They're together now, as if they're climbing. I see our two Thomases climbing."

My brother Thomas was literally crazy about climbing. I'm troubled by this image and I say this to Dominique, who cannot help but be surprised herself by the clarity of what she's capturing. Dominique's son passed away from leukemia in 2001, the same year as my brother. The sickness took him away in fifteen days. How can a mother even conceive of her son's imminent death? How does a medium experience the death of someone so close to them? Had she known it would happen? Does she communicate with him?

Today Dominique believes that a part of her always knew that her son would depart early. But of course it was never something she thought about. "It would have driven me insane!" she says. She did not realize this until she looked back. Since then, Dominique has seen many mothers who have experienced the same thing she went through. And even though these women are not mediums themselves, they often share with her that very peculiar feeling: "Deep down, I knew it would happen."

Outside of this kind of premonitory intuition, which one doesn't realize until afterwards has existed for years, Dominique had the sense and the luck to be spared. A part of her brain knew, but she never felt any anger at not having been warned. What would it have changed, other than driving her crazy? Her mediumship, in this case, did not make her a different mother.

The loss of a child is an infinite suffering, one that is inextinguishable. Dominique does not keep a single photo of her son on the walls in her house. She is incapable of looking at them, but when her Thomas left she very quickly witnessed things that helped her understand that he was still present. She had tremendous numbers of signs, some of which she doesn't even talk about because they would seem so insane. One more than the others remains engraved in her memory. One day in March, the windows were wide open in her bedroom, and while Dominique was holding a drawing by Thomas in her hands and asking him to give her a sign, at that very moment a swallow came into the bedroom and immediately went back out again. This surprise moved her deeply, but it was nothing compared to what happened a few hours later: when she arrived at the cemetery, on top of Thomas's grave she discovered . . . the lifeless body of a dead swallow. She remembers having been gripped and overwhelmed by emotion.

Such synchronicities are relatively commonplace in the case of grieving, to the point that several research programs have studied it, with extremely shocking results.[6] A synchronicity assumes a prominent emotional significance for the person who experiences it, because it is the objective and indisputable acknowledgment of a link of meaning between different elements or episodes in one's life, links that are not attributable to the law of cause and effect. This subtle distinction tells rational people that signs can be seen wherever they want them to be, and that it is by chance that they happen. Therefore, it would have been by chance that Dominique asked for a sign from her son and saw a swallow come into her bedroom at the same moment, and that she found one dead on the grave in the afternoon. Of course. But sometimes, over time, even the most Cartesian thinkers discover that our feelings, our subjective perceptions, are at times more accurate than our scientific certainties. This is the case for me. In fact, in my endless questioning since my brother's death, I have discovered that it is sometimes irrational to avoid so many signs on the pretext of wanting to remain rational.

Did Dominique's mediumship help her in her grief? Yes, even though the loss of a child is a wound that never closes. One can never finish grieving for a child. Every year, she imagines him one year older. Would he perhaps be married today? Would she have been a grandmother? The mom in her, the woman, is not the medium. She is amputated for life. This being said, when mothers come to see her, she understands what is impossible to understand for those who have not been through such an ordeal. She knows that she has to move on, help people, and not let herself go. There are women who fall apart, and this is not in Dominique's nature.

---

6   See Stéphane Allix and Paul Bernstein (eds.), *Expériences extraordinaires. Le manuel clinique*, Dunod/InterEditions, 2013.

The day of the funeral, in shock, she didn't shed a single tear, not one, to the point that she was even bothered by it.

No, mediumship does not heal. This comment by Dominique is important to remember, because we will explore it further at the end of this book, when we discuss the potential role that a consultation with a medium can play in a grieving process. On the other hand, mediumship does help her by giving her the certainty that she will see her son again. This is the only thing of which she is totally convinced: she will see him again. Sometimes she hears him, too. Those moments are times of great peace. This doesn't happen every day, far from it, only when Thomas has things to tell his mother. She repeats that she doesn't like looking at photos of him because those images bring her back to the past, to the pain. When she hears him, though, he is an adult. He is the person he has become today.

She says she has been able to move on thanks to the support of her son, and to the feeling that she is useful to the mothers she sees who are grieving. She refuses to feel like a victim of injustice. What injustice? God's? Because her son is dead? No.

In a process of grieving, going to see a medium is not a necessity. But if the idea takes shape in a person's spirit, it shouldn't be suppressed, either, for it could become an extremely precious support. A consultation may be able to open a small door, Dominique says, but she also warns that in no case should a person imagine that a séance will sort out a person's suffering: mediumship is not a magic painkiller.

Consequently, like the other mediums I know, she recommends not going to too many consultations. Seeing a medium every three months does nothing. Quite the reverse, in fact; waiting is necessary to allow time for a new relationship to be constructed. A different relationship that integrates the person's absence. Maintaining an artificial and unchanged relationship with the deceased by using the medium as an intermediary, believing that the deceased person can be communicated with, is not therapeutic in the long-term. It can even become an obstacle to well-being.

And our well-being influences that of our deceased loved ones. Dominique has observed many times, actually, that when the people who come to see her become calm, the deceased also become calm.

Consultation with a medium is not incompatible with the support of a psychologist; quite the contrary. You just have to find a therapist who will know not to make unfair judgements. Or don't talk about it with them if you are afraid of their reaction. One of my close friends felt obligated not to tell his therapist that he had gone to see a medium with his wife after the death of their child. It was difficult for him because the therapist was very helpful, but so was the consultation with the medium. It had perhaps even saved his life.

Another activity that a medium may be involved in still concerns the deceased. Not those we are close to and for whom we come to consultations, but rather the people nobody thinks about anymore. When she first begins her work as a medium, conducting contact séances with the deceased, Dominique is called by people who are facing problems at home, problems they attribute to entities that have remained in place and who need to be kindly asked to leave. Dominique comes out of these experiences convinced that such presences are able to deeply disturb a human being. A person might feel tired, for example; they might notice that things are going inexplicably terribly. These entities are actually a little like energetic vampires; they feed off of the energy of the people living in the houses they occupy, even if they clearly no longer have a place there. This rather alarming idea has been alluded to in well-known films like *The Sixth Sense* and *The Others*. Still, based on what Dominique is saying, these phenomena are entirely real. But who are these entities, and why do they remain in houses?

One of the most remarkable experiences Dominique has ever had took place in Orgeval, not far from Paris. It starts with a phone call from a woman renting a property in the town, which is in north-central France, who feels that something in the house is not right. This is the reason she has called Dominique. It sounds like the situation is taking on a worrying dimension: every member of her family is falling without any explanation. The husband, the daughters, and the mother. The mother says she suffers from constant migraines. When Dominique arrives at the property, she has barely entered before she is taken hold of by the strange atmosphere and has to sit down. "I thought I was going to throw up. Yes, there was a problem in that house," she remembers.

Once she has recovered from her initial reaction, she goes farther into the house and abruptly sees children appear. It's a sight that is difficult to describe, but one that for her has the force of a real event. "What happened with children in this house?" she asks the occupants. They don't know, but they promise to find out. Continuing on, Dominique then sees a well, and in the well, she discovers horror.

She is so overwhelmed that she decides to keep this vision from the occupants so that they do not panic even more. Dominique returns home filled with the pain she perceived at the house. She feels that the house was the setting of an enormous suffering that involved children to an unbearable degree. So she begins to pray. She speaks to those children, asking them to leave the place where they are not doing well. That is not their place.

She returns to the house two days later. In the meantime, her clients were able to speak with their neighbor, who has lived in Orgeval longer than they have. They tell Dominique that their house sheltered children in the public assistance program. Placed there in the 1950s, the poor little ones were not well fed or properly cared for, and they endured violence from a deplorable woman who, under the guise of taking them in, made them live in hell. In addition to this maltreatment, the rumor was that children had died.

Now Dominique better understands: the enormous mass of sorrow had transformed into an egregore of suffering. An egregore is a psychic force generated by the emotions of several people, and it is a force that can manifest itself as a kind of entity with autonomous behavior. In that house in Orgeval, that mass of clinging energy was soaking into the walls and mixing with the souls of children wandering there. Dominique is certain that children died in that house and were thrown in the well or buried in the basement. Those little souls, whose bodies never received any grave, had stayed there because no love had shone on them.

After praying once at her house, and having spoken with sweetness, kindness, and love to the children, Dominique has the feeling that they have left, as if the simple act of talking to them in this way has been enough to make them understand that they have no obligation to be there. A few gentle words, imbued with a little love, have freed them. For Dominique, in fact, an entity, more than anything else, is a soul who is not all right and who needs to leave. When the soul is eventually able to hear this, whether through its own evolution, through the intervention of a medium, or even a kind person speaking to it or offering their prayers, it manages to break free from the places where it finds itself stuck. Since then, the house in Orgeval and the family who lives in it have found peace again, as have the children's souls.

A somewhat similar episode takes place on a large property in the Limoges region. A couple of sheep farmers make a call to Dominique one day about the proliferation of bizarre phenomena they have noticed in a field they have just acquired to enlarge their pasture area. When they are there, the sheep behave erratically, lose their appetites, and the mothers abandon their lambs, several of which have died; the grown sheep are also dying. Generally speaking, no one feels right in that field. Even the equipment has problems: the tractor constantly breaks down when it enters the plot of land.

When she connects with this spot, Dominique sees monks and painful events that left a mark on the ground. After some research, the farmers learn that a monastic community lived here centuries ago, quite a large community, one that thrived independently. They raised livestock, grew their own grains, and made their own wine. The plague decimated the congregation. No one came to help them. All of the monks died in terrible suffering. The last ones to die were probably not buried, of course. Time passed, but those souls never left the place. Dominique explains that the upheavals noticed by everyone else were kinds of calls for help from these souls. Why this way? How? She has no idea, but from the instant that she detects these presences and understands what has happened, just as she had done for the children, she blends prayers with offers to help and allows them to free themselves.

What should we think about these two stories? The troubling fact is that these are not the only such stories I have heard. All of the mediums and other sensitives I have met over the years attest to similar events. And they all put forward the same diagnosis: even when the unexplained manifestations are distressing and worrying, the large majority of the time they indicate the presence of lost souls that are stuck inside their fears, *but that are not evil*. Let's leave that for the

B movies. These souls are terrified and need help, light, and love. The results usually obtained through medium interventions are positive.

These results are sometimes quite spectacular, and other times nothing dramatic really happens. This could be because the person intervening is not competent. We may also be dealing with a charlatan. In this domain, like in any other, we encounter as many deliberately malevolent people as we do innocent people, without discernment, who believe they are doing the right thing. The psychology of the inhabitants of a "haunted" house is also a fascinating part of the resolution, or lack thereof, of these phenomena. It may even be, in certain cases, that this psychology is not unrelated to their occurrence.

When I mention the psychology of a place's inhabitants, I'm not talking about people who invent things or play practical jokes. No, what I'm addressing here is a rather mysterious area of the human psyche where, to put it simply, nothing happens by chance.

Broadly speaking, what I mean is that errant souls, houses, and their current occupants sometimes form an indissociable whole. Why do we one day arrive at a certain house? Why do we feel drawn to that one rather than somewhere else? Do certain houses *call* us? Why does the past of a place we are living in, when it is revealed, seem to have so many similarities with our own past? Why do some places seem familiar to us even though we are setting foot in them for the first time? Why do the same things happen to people who live in the same place later? These are some of the many questions that examine our conscious and unconscious ties with the invisible world we are swimming in. These ties may have a thousand different origins: our history, our ancestors, our weaknesses, our flaws, our psychic dispositions, etc. This idea, which scientific parapsychology and different schools of innovative psychology have been working on for decades, and which so many psychologists from INREES[7] have explored for several years, is an absolutely fascinating area of research. The fact is that what has been observed must be considered.

To get back to wandering souls, like the children or the monks, could it be that among the people who have been dead for centuries, there are some who have not realized it has happened?

Has my father realized that he is dead?

It makes sense, after all: if death does not exist and life continues on, how do we know we have died? Do we wake up in death as if we're coming out of a long dream? Or is it the opposite, as if we are diving into an endless dream? Out of all the people who die every day, how many of them find themselves in states of great confusion and are transformed into wandering souls?

Dominique assures me that since the large majority of people today die in hospitals, the end-of-life process gives them enough time to get used to the idea. The examples of the children or monks are extreme cases. It would seem that the way we die influences our arrival into death, and theirs must not have been joyful. One can imagine that a person who has been murdered would be more inclined to ask for help to find peace than an old lady who slowly passed away in her bed. Dominique describes a sort of continuity, a similarity between the circumstances of the end of life, the dying, and the first steps on the other side. There is no magic wand to go from an abominable life to an existence that is full of serenity in death. This is the reason it is best to chip away at

---

7   Institute for Research on Extraordinary Experiences, www.inrees.com.

our issues and to work to fix the problems we have while we are alive to prevent them from poisoning us once we are on the other side.

Nevertheless, we may be holding onto a reading that is too literal. There are so many details that escape us; let's not forget this important point. Dominique in fact warns me that this schema is not invariable. If a kind of psychological continuity seems to exist between life, death, and the after-death—which is a concept we find almost without fail in several traditions all across the world—Dominique has already seen cases where people who had a terrible end to their life experienced light and peace after their passage to the other side.

Death, like life, is also a space of redemption, evolution, and growth. Nothing, anywhere, is fixed in eternity. And there are also beings who help us.

If death slightly resembles what we had during our lifetime, it is also very different from it. We no longer have a body, but what are the other changes? Who do we become when we die? Do we arrive in a world similar to our own, where we can run into other people? These questions still seem largely unreachable to me. Like Henry, Dominique suggests the existence of different vibratory planes. We find ourselves on one or another as a function of what we were when we were alive. The deceased sometimes mention landscapes, very beautiful landscapes, but beyond that? Does death have to remain invisible to the living?

The final part of my consultation with Dominique will be, in this regard, one of the most extraordinary events I was able to experience during these tests. As with Henry, my father is demonstrating his presence during the séance, I cannot deny that. Still, he's taking a while to tell me what I put in the casket. And this is becoming incomprehensible. Could it have something to do with the state in which he finds himself now? Dominique is able to contact him, though.

"He's a very discreet man, your dad. He gave me his respiratory problem, his reserve, his art . . . He has somewhat of a stern side to him, too. He has a fairly linear life apart from his travels. He's pretty structured, direct, honest."

Yes, all of that is correct, but in the same way that it happened with Henry, I don't understand why my father is not saying what I'm expecting him to. Just a few words: what I put in his casket. The silence on this point is a mystery. Why doesn't he say anything himself, spontaneously? I believe I now have to carefully lead Dominique into the area we're interested in.

"What can he describe to me about the end of his life, his funeral, that whole period in general?"

"He says the end of his life was long, he was at the end of his rope. It's annoying, he must have been torn in two because he was going to leave his wife and that, for him, was a tragedy. It's obvious, but . . . your dad is a man who has a hard time talking. I can really tell, as soon as it goes toward something sensitive, he stops me."

"All right, but he has things to tell me. Does he know what I'm talking about?"

"Is it something that might affect his restraint? Because if that's the case, we're going to find ourselves blocked."

I am really getting the feeling that my targeting is having a reverse effect. Dominique feels as if she is under pressure. On the other hand, she notices that my father is objecting as soon as the conversation turns toward a sensitive topic. We're not out of the woods yet. But finally he begins to talk about his burial.

"Was there a kind of orchestra, a . . . what happened exactly? There was something special at his burial?"

"What are you sensing?"

"That there had been an orchestra or someone who sang something for him."

"Someone played the flute for him."

"I was feeling that there was something a little special. But as soon as we go toward emotion he keeps wanting to put me back in front of more cheerful things: 'Okay, both of you stop it right now with all this stuff and nonsense!'"

"But he still needs to give me some details, he knows this. I talk to him about it all the time."

"If he really wants to answer us, I'm the channel. I can't do anything if he doesn't want to."

"I am well aware that this creates a kind of tension for you."

"Have you already done this several times?"

Dominique is asking me if I have already gone to see other mediums to communicate with my father. She doesn't know anything about the other participants or the order of the different consultations.

"Yes."

"Honestly, that's what I was afraid of: when we request something from the deceased several times, even if your father is very kind, there comes a time when they can say stop."

"Sure, but I also have the feeling that he is really a part of this experiment, and I don't feel like I'm forcing his hand."

"All right."

"He knows how important this book is. Not just for me, but also for the people who will read it . . . And honestly, I swear that I don't understand. It's been clear to me from the beginning of the séance that there's an open connection between the two of you: when you take your breaths like him, the way you describe his personality and other things . . . At the same time, there are also questions I'd like to ask him, and I feel like if I ask them, I can't get the answers. In your opinion, why is it difficult to ask him questions?"

"Because what you're asking isn't what's most important! What's essential is what he's telling us, the private things he's giving spontaneously: the end of his life, his problems breathing, his regrets, the way he suffered for Thomas. You see? This is his way of identifying himself to us. Now, I can understand the fact that you have questions that are important to you, and we can ask them, we'll see. He'll answer or he won't, but I can't go hunting for a response."

"Something happened when he was put in the casket, something I asked him to remember and relay to a medium. It's like a game: 'If there is life after death, when you die, say this to a medium . . .'"

"Ah, okay, and are there other people who found the answer?"

"Don't put any pressure on yourself, Dominique. And don't hesitate to tell me if any images come to you, even if to you they seem completely ridiculous."

"Yes . . . well, well, I'm kinda running out of steam here."

"Are you not picking anything up or is it because you're feeling apprehensive?"

"It's kind of a trap, you see, I'm putting up barriers. Your father has already made me so emotional that now it's not even that I'm going to make a mistake, it's that I don't have anything . . . I don't have any concrete sentences to give you."

I probably didn't explain myself properly, because Dominique thinks I'm asking my father to say a sentence intended for me. I suddenly imagine the tension she is feeling, considering that obtaining a single word is sometime so arduous.

"Maybe your emotion is blocking you from putting things together?"

"No . . . well, yes, maybe, that could be part of it. But your dad was so nice to me that now, since I don't have anything, I wonder if maybe all of this is not very important for him."

"Am I asking too much?"

"Yes, that's what I'm telling you."

"I don't mean from him, but from you."

"No, I think it has to do with him. See, if he had not been precise during the séance, I would have been a little annoyed. Because vagueness, as a medium, is not possible. In a good consultation we should get precise details in which we can find the deceased. We can't be content with ordinary phrases like: 'He's doing well, your father loves you.' But now, it's as if there are limits. I feel it, as though we were punted away. You saw that he talked about the funeral, then you ask me a question and all of a sudden, nothing. This doesn't mean that it doesn't exist up there, but maybe he just doesn't find it fundamentally important. Do you see what I mean?"

"Yes, and I'm noticing that when I communicate with him through you or with another medium, it's not the same as if I were talking with my father the way we used to. There are new parameters, and that's what I'm trying to explore a bit, that's what I'm trying to understand. Because when you tell me that it's not important to him, I still have a little bit of trouble believing it."

"So for you, it is important?"

"For me it is, and—knowing my father—I know that it's important to him, too. But we can stop here if you want."

"Yes, okay, but do you understand why as a medium I had a hard time clicking with you? Because I'm very happy about the contact I made with your dad."

"Yes, so am I."

"It bothers me a little that I couldn't find it . . . but oh well. Thanks, Jean-Pierre."

I end the recording, and we continue talking about various things. I still don't reveal anything else to Dominique. Like the other mediums, she will not have a second chance to complete her séance. In fact, like the other mediums—and like you—she will not discover the nature of the test until she reads this book.

Before leaving her house, I nevertheless decide to risk it all and reveal one final detail to her: "I didn't ask my father to say a sentence to you, but I placed something in his casket and told him: 'The day I go to see a medium, tell them what it was.'"

"I thought you had asked him to repeat a sentence for us."

"I was trying to say things in a way that wouldn't give too much direction."

"Is it something drawn?"

"Is that what's coming to you?"

"Something drawn, like a comic book or . . . a little like a notebook, I don't know . . . that's the image I'm getting."

"Try to describe to me what you see."

"A small children's notebook or something he had you read . . . Is that it?"

Let's recall that in the casket I had placed the novel my father had had me read: *The Tartar Steppe*. But Dominique also mentions a drawing, a notebook.

"I can't tell you."

". . . Because that could be tied to the child," she continues. "It could be tied to something, a drawing book, a notebook with drawings on it."

"What's happening right now, are you seeing images or is he talking to you?"

"A book? A drawing, a notebook, a notepad, a small thing

like that? That's what I'm seeing. That's what he's sending me, it's . . . or he's just teasing me, if that's not what it is."

This is the first time she has mentioned a "book." I can tell she's turning it over, she's getting warmer, but between what she's seeing fuzzily and the way that her brain interprets it, confusion slips in. Her own confusion or my father's? What is my father doing while all of this is happening? Is he the one who once again can't manage to make himself understood? All the same, keep in mind that the copy of *The Tartar Steppe* that I slid into my father's casket was a paperback . . . a small format that might evoke the image of a notepad.

"Why can't my father speak to you using his voice?"

"What I pick up comes to me either as clairaudience—his voice that I'm hearing—or as clairvoyance, an image he sends me. Right now I'm seeing more images. So did he make a mistake? Have we had some pollution?"

"Pollution? What are you talking about?"

"Interference. But if he wants to come, he'll come, I trust him . . . I don't know if it's a book, this is annoying . . . What was I saying? Yes, if he thinks it would be helpful for him to come, he will come."

Another mention of a book, it's unbelievable. I'm so intrigued that this is happening like this. And since I'm not helping Dominique at all by saying whether or not what she is saying is correct, she has the sensation of turning in a circle, not stopping at any of the details she sees.

"Your dad has told us something. He's so sensitive, so kind, that, well, if I don't find what you put in his casket, it's not that big a deal in the end."

"No, and besides, maybe it will come to you tonight."

"Oh, I don't know: a paintbrush, drawing paper, tube of color, with landscapes, voilà."

No! Why is this happening now? Is this a joke? I can't believe it! Dominique drops this information so nonchalantly, but someone definitely just came and whispered it in her ear. I try not to reveal my excitement. My father barely managed to get across the vague idea of a book to Dominique, and now, as if it were nothing, "paintbrush," "tube of color!" And not in a list of fifty words where they might have found a match by chance—no, in this sentence: "Paintbrush, drawing paper, tube of color . . ."

"Is that what's coming in now? What you just said, were you joking?"

"No, it came to me . . . You know, sometimes it comes like that, spontaneously. I sometimes obtain extremely accurate information that someone has waited for unsuccessfully throughout the séance that the deceased decides to give when the client is leaving, about to walk out the door. You can't stop it, you can't cut the line. You see, your father is going to follow you when you leave."

Yes, and he has also just accurately named two of the four objects that I put in his casket while I was in the process of ending the interview! And this after also managing to make the image of the book appear to Dominique . . .

On my way back to Paris, I am in shock.

Was my father playing with me? Or was he doing battle with the medium's tense mind and then taking advantage of Dominique's relaxation and lowered apprehension, once the séance was officially over, to express himself?

And to think that I can't share my astonishment with anyone else. I have seen two mediums and two have passed the test. Not in the way I expected, but isn't it true that I was able to learn so much precisely because of how it ended up happening? I am so shaken to feel my father here with me! What I am living right now is so amazing. I can't really comprehend it.

So, Papa, shall we continue?

Christelle

Christelle Dubois moved to Brittany with her small family a few years ago. With her husband Sébastien, she welcomes me into their house located on the edge of a village. Their two children, a boy and a girl, are at school.

This is the first time I am meeting Christelle. We have corresponded periodically, particularly on the subject of the testing she had conducted in Toulouse with Dr. Jean-Jacques Charbonier, which we have summarized in the *Inexploré*[8] magazine, but we have never crossed paths. Dr. Charbonier, an anesthetist specializing in near-death experiences, had welcomed her to his hospital to test a medium in an attempt to enter into contact with people in a coma (I will return later to this incredible collaboration). When Christelle and I spoke on the phone, I could tell she was someone rational, with both feet on the ground, and that she was also very reassuring.

As I walk through the door, I sense that she is delighted to meet me and to be participating in the test, and at the same time she seems very restless. Honestly, here I was thinking that the fact that I've been working on the subject of death for years, and that I am familiar with mediumship, would make the mediums more relaxed, less worried about being trapped, but in fact the reverse is true. They are all stressed.

---

8   *Inexploré*, no 18, spring 2013.

Probably because we are both impatient to begin, we start the séance very quickly. Sébastien disappears. In the hour that follows, I have to admit that I feel more and more strongly that my father is present. It is really very hard to describe this sensation because it is new for me. I am aware of my expectations, my desire for the test to work a third time, and I know how much this hope might be influencing my feelings. But this is not the case. I am very vigilant about this. And I *feel* that he is here.

This budding sensation is more and more objective for me, particularly as it has been reinforced by the positive results of the first two tests: my father is really a key player in these experiments.

In front of me, two beings are trying to enter into contact. To do this, they must both make a significant effort, the medium on the side of the living and my father in the beyond. It's not a question of magic, religion, or belief in a Hollywood fantasy. All of this is genuinely real.

As I did with Dominique Vallée, I immediately slide the photo of my father onto the table. Christelle finds him instantly.

"He's coming with a hat . . . and lots of landscapes. He's drawing lots of landscapes, there are a lot of colors. He's not coming by himself, though. There is a second man next to him, someone who left quite a while ago. He's a person who really loved to travel. But not necessarily physically. The part he liked about traveling also has to do with culture . . . He's talking about his wife . . . is she still alive?"

"Yes."

As I said, because my father was a painter and taught geography, the earth and its landscapes were a delight to him.

He had taken several grand adventurous journeys, most notably to Iran and Afghanistan in the fifties. Then, later, his dreams about traveling became more significant than the trips themselves. Less disappointing, too, probably. As he got older, he also revealed to us the names of places that he had fantasized about so intensely when, as a young man, he used to dream while looking at the pages of an atlas—names like "Central Asia" or "Taklamakan Desert," etc.—which, when he was fully grown, formed the reflections of a bygone time. So what good did it do to move? A man of travel, yes, but "not necessarily physically." Christelle's remark is astonishing and pertinent. But he's moved on to his wife, my mother.

"You need to take care of her. She misses him enormously. He's making a motion as if he were putting his hand on top of hers. He regrets not having reassured her . . . all right . . . someone thought about him recently . . . This is your father?"

"Yes."

"He's telling me that his legs hurt him toward the end. He doesn't like illness, he doesn't like getting old . . . He's grumbling, complaining a little bit about the end of his life. As if the end of his life hadn't been what he had imagined it would be. That's not the way he saw it happening . . . Did he lose his head a little bit? He didn't really know where he was at the very end of his life, did he? He's saying very firmly, 'That was not okay with me! I didn't like that one bit!'"

Around ten days before his departure, something very strange and quite unpleasant for all of us happened. Though he was exhausted by his illness, my father could not manage to sleep. Without our knowledge, and thinking they were doing the right thing, the staff member caring for him gave him a sleeping pill. This small pill had an extremely violent hallucinogenic effect on my father. In the middle of the night, thinking he was in danger, he tore apart his IV and everything around him on the bed. To keep him from hurting himself, the nurses tied him down, as they were unable to remain constantly at his bedside. My mother alerted me in the morning, and I came immediately.

The horror.

This man who was so wise, so kind, so polite, so cultured, who had shown so much kindness to other people all his life, was tied to his bed as if he were insane.

This picture of him, his disbelieving gaze, still follows me.

I had barely come into the room before I removed his constraints. I freed his hands and legs, threw the straps far out of sight, and promised him that this would never, ever happen to him again. He looked at me as if he felt a little lost.

Even hours later, he was still having trouble coming back to himself. In that instant, my brother Simon, my mother, and I decided to no longer leave him alone, even for a moment. We would take turns spending the days and especially the nights with him. Our determination and the professionalism of the staff caring for him were such that this did not pose the slightest problem. A mattress was added in a corner of the room. We took care of him in a way that my brother and I had never thought we were capable of doing. This was an intense time, but we were happy to be there and to do our part. My father, who had been so reserved throughout his life, released his body to us. I doubt that he enjoyed feeling so helpless in his last weeks. So yes, "he lost his head a little bit, he didn't really know where he was at the very end of his life," all of this is exactly right.

Christelle doesn't know this. But she insists.

"He didn't like being infantilized, he knew it wasn't done on purpose, that it was out of love, but he didn't like it. He felt ridiculous . . . He doesn't like his body at the end . . . Charlie, do you know a Charlie?"

"No," I say, surprised that now we've jumped from one thing to another.

"He's saying, 'My Charlie.'"

"I don't get it."

I don't understand what this name could be related to. There is no Charles or Charlie in my father's family.

"OK, I don't understand what he's saying, he's very focused on his past, this man. He says he's close with you, and even if it's not easy for him, he's coming because you asked a great deal of him and there are things you're waiting for."

The clarity with which Christelle captures all of these details is impressive. And here's my father letting her know that I'm expecting something from him. This is a confirmation on his part that he is aware of the test we are performing. I am only half-surprised that he is saying this is not easy for him.

"But this isn't his thing," Christelle continues, "he's not very focused on his life . . . um . . . did he lose a brother?"

"No, not that I know of."

"Because I have two men next to him, and one of them is giving me the sense of being his brother. It's important to him that he sorts everything out pertaining to the family, because it was complicated."

What a strange question. My father was an only child. It is known in the family that his mother had had several miscarriages before he was born, and that she had to remain on bedrest for part of her pregnancy while she was waiting to have my father. But to our knowledge, no other child was born. And as far as I know, nothing in our family could be described as "complicated." If I'm pausing on this point, it's for the following reason, and it is this most recent detail that is extremely troubling: two of the next three mediums who are participating in the test will also mention the existence of this brother my father might have had. One of these mediums will also receive a name: Charles. The same one given to Christelle!

The coincidence is so unlikely that I will throw myself into unending research about my family. It is still under way.

Sometimes, these kinds of experiences lead us onto paths we didn't expect. To this day, I have not found a trace of another child born to my paternal grandparents. But I am still disturbed by the fact that three mediums indicated the possible existence of this brother.

Christelle Dubois is a somewhat unique medium. In fact, this young thirty-three-year-old woman works as a nurse's aide. Her two professions are blending together for the moment, neither one taking precedence over the other. One foot in the world of the dead—whom she does not like to qualify as "dead," by the way, because they aren't—and another in the hospital. Listening to her tell me about her childhood, I feel like I'm listening to Henry or Dominique.

From a very young age, she does indeed see people at the foot of her bed. They are there, then they disappear like soap bubbles. She doesn't know what it means; she's too little to understand that what she's seeing is abnormal. In reality, like tens of thousands of other little girls and boys around the world, she is just more sensitive than other children. But this is part of her. Nothing sensational. It's so normal that she doesn't even feel the need to talk about it.

Also, no one is telling her that the people she is seeing are dead. And since this is something she can't tell by seeing, she is not afraid. These visions happen most often in her bedroom when she wakes up. Someone is at the foot of her bed, not moving, or sometimes touching her feet. A silhouette, sometimes several, men and women, even children. Often the same characters come back. All of this is like a dream. It's part of her reality. Then, as she gets older, Christelle starts to hear the voices of these beings who until now were immobile and silent. Calls for help. Messages they're asking her to pass on.

It is also at a young age that her desire to become a nurse's aide or nurse emerges. She is not even ten years old and is already fascinated by the technical side of medicine. She sees herself working in intensive care, in the operating room. She loves visiting hospitals to visit her sick grandfather or whenever she has the chance.

As an adolescent, she represses her mediumship. She cuts off and refuses her perceptions. At the time, she manages to do this in the moment; no one teaches her how to put herself in a "non-receptive" mode. Even if she receives information or hears voices in her head, she no longer pays them any attention, like when someone is talking next to you and you pointedly ignore them. The technique becomes more refined over time, and will serve her well later when she enters the medical field.

Not entering into inner dialogue. Putting up barriers. Talking normally while, at the same time, they are talking inside her head. As she listens to them, she begins to speak with her small inner voice and says: "Be quiet, I don't want to hear you," or: "Excuse me, but I can't." Typically, Christelle says, after a while she no longer hears them.

She doesn't decide to "reopen" everything until the age of twenty-four, after the birth of her daughter, during which a hemorrhage puts her on the brink of death. When she realizes afterward that she barely avoided that catastrophe, what surprises her is that she felt protected during the birth, even at the worst moments. She had been spared the anxiety, even the pain. So she wants to say thank you. And the only way to do it seems suddenly obvious to her: to accept the voices she is hearing, and accept her perceptions as a medium.

Everything returns. Even better than before, more focused.

But she nevertheless steers herself toward caring for others. She starts with small jobs as a caregiver, then passes the certification for nurse's aide, even though she is already the mother of two children. She struggles, but as she says, "We can't have something for nothing." Her husband Sébastien is supportive. Her perceptions? They are a part of his life, too. He has had the chance several times to realize that what his wife sees is not imaginary, especially when she gives him information coming to him from his deceased loved ones.

What about the children? She avoids talking about it too much with them because if they too are called to develop a kind of sensitivity, she wants them to have their own experience of the beyond. However, when an animal dies, she sensitizes them to death. To the fact that we can still accompany a being that goes away. That it's not terrible, that it's part of life. If she talks about anything with her husband—the deceased she sees in their bedroom, for example—she is very careful that it is never in front of the children.

With her nurse's aide diploma in hand, her first job leads her to . . . a palliative care unit. There she will see souls.

At the hospital, as Christelle had already noticed during her internships, she *senses* the patients. Whether they are alive or not, when they arrive in the unit, she knows what is wrong with them without even needing to check their charts. Her abilities increase further when she performs their daily care routine or helps them wash themselves, for example. As soon as she makes physical contact with the person, she dives into their soul.

What's more, when she works at night, the atmosphere is conducive to mediumship. Less noise, less moving around, and the energies are gentler. During the day there is a lot of electricity in the air, but at night it's as if a kind of bubble appears that allows mediumship to be felt more easily. At night, people open up with greater ease.

Christelle will work in many different units. She acts as a substitute. But she always remains extremely discreet about her perceptions, even if sometimes she lets out a few clues. Christelle cares a great deal about cleaning the dead for burial, and can spend two hours doing this while her colleagues would only need ten minutes. This is because in addition to the work she has to do, she is very attentive to the soul of the person she is taking care of: does it have anything to tell her? Does it need anything in particular?

Like that grandfather who one day requests his suspenders and his béret. The man had died in the middle of the night. But his preparation for burial could not be performed because it was a busy night and Christelle and her colleague had other residents to take care of. In the morning, when the new team arrives, Christelle tells her day colleague that she definitely wants to perform the cleaning. They start taking care of the man together. But the day aide is annoyed. The shift is starting off quite full for her, and now, having just come in, she has to take care of a mortuary cleaning.

While they both busy themselves over the old man's body, Christelle suddenly hears the deceased tell her: "Don't forget my suspenders and my béret." She doesn't pay attention at first because, she says, sometimes caregivers speak into the void, or make jokes. Then the voice comes back: "Make sure you put on my béret and my suspenders." So Christelle picks up the bag containing the clothes brought by the family. She doesn't know what's inside. She finds a suit that has just come from the dry cleaner's. The voice again: "Don't forget the suspenders and the béret." So she tells her colleague that they need to find the suspenders and the béret.

Her colleague looks at her without any particular reaction. "Okay, sure, if you want."

When she finds the suspenders beneath the suit, her colleague starts looking at Christelle strangely. When the man is dressed, Christelle looks at the bottom of the bag and finds a small sealable plastic sack . . . containing the béret. This time her colleague is dumbstruck. And the man is quite happy.

Christelle doesn't really respond to her colleague's worried question ("Did you look in the bag?"—she hadn't) and evades it with a burst of laughter. "Oh, I'll explain it to you."

Christelle will reveal a little more to another colleague, but this time by accident. During another mortuary cleaning, Christelle abruptly asks her to be careful when she's moving the person around. The other responds that the person is dead. Then, a little irritated by this lack of respect, Christelle reveals to her that she can speak with the deceased. At first the other woman doesn't react. They will not speak about it again for several days, until they share an experience. At the time, a flu epidemic had brought in several people in a relatively short period of time. That day, during another mortuary preparation for a lady who had just died, the deceased appears by stirring up a large gust of air in the room, even though all of the windows and the door are closed. At the same time, both nurse's aides have tears in their eyes as if they have just experienced something with a very powerful energy, not knowing what it is; well, actually, Christelle *does* know. Stupefied, her colleague looks at her and says, "Okay, now I believe you, I believe you. You can talk to the dead!" They have been friends since then.

Apart from that moment, even if Christelle is taking care of patients as a nurse's aide and does not close herself off from her mediumship, to the teams she works with, she is still a colleague like any other, and she does not bring up the subject.

Does mediumship help her with her work? In certain situations, definitely. But it can also complicate what she is doing because it slows her down so much. She is aware that she takes longer with her care for patients at the end of their lives. She knows they are there, and wants to make sure they are all right, sometimes even staying an extra ten minutes in the room. In the world of nursing, death is ordinary, Christelle remarks. We don't take the time to think about it and don't even dare to talk about it. One must remain neutral, supposedly. At the same time, which is paradoxical, the nurse's aides, nurses, and hospital staff, all of these people in contact with patients, have anecdotes about unexplainable experiences. But each one remains quiet in their corner. Nobody shares these stories, even though there are many of them. The wall of silence is not impossible to cross over, but it's still fairly high.

Does Christelle ever have moments of doubt? Not about the reality that she perceives. However, she has wondered for a long time about how she can explain her perceptions. She is sure of one thing: no, it is not her imagination playing tricks on her. For one thing, the countless confirmations she has received throughout her life indicate that she is picking up accurate information that does not come from her, like the grandfather's suspenders and béret. What's more, she *feels* when she is starting to extrapolate. When she perceives something as a medium, she has the sense that she is no longer in charge of her mind. The information arrives whether she wants it to or not.

She also gets messages sometimes that are not in line with her own values or thoughts, that actually are against her way of being. And there is that voice she hears and that she cannot control. It's not her mind, it's a voice that from time to time has peculiar intonations. Sometimes, for instance, it is a very broken voice when she is communicating with someone who underwent a tracheotomy at the end of their life—a detail that she learns afterwards.

Could this be a kind of telepathy? Here, again, Christelle is familiar with this feeling, since she uses telepathy today to communicate with people suffering from Alzheimer's. She is also able to very easily tell the difference between telepathy and communication with the deceased. With telepathy, she says she *hears* the information in the area of her forehead, while the deceased speak into her ear or just behind her head. Telepathy also is not really a voice, but images, and in these cases she is not feeling the energy of the deceased: in the case of communication with a disembodied entity, Christelle says she feels a unique energy, an energy of someone who has passed. In communications with the beyond, she goes through several stages and she feels "this very distinctive energy . . . I sense a *source.*"

But she has noticed that as soon as she is asked a specific question during a séance, she has the feeling of toppling over in her mind. As if she has fallen down. Then she has to re-learn to free herself to return to her medium side. But this is difficult to do. She asks to see. She needs to be poised, then she asks internally to receive whatever it is she will receive. As if she were pulling out her earplugs and making herself available. She is able to do this instantaneously.

I will also discover that ideally, once she is in this state, she almost doesn't want to be asked any questions at all as she lets the messages come from the deceased.

Back to Brittany. Christelle has mentioned my father's mysterious brother, but both she and my father have already moved onto something else.

"He's talking about the small wool blanket he had on his hospital bed that had come with him from home. That was very good for him, and gave him a lot of reassurance."

My parents had brought that blanket back from Afghanistan, where they had gone after Thomas's death. My mother had brought it to the hospital for him because my father quite liked it. He died wrapped up in it.

"Your dad is talking about a lot of things, it's like we've pierced through a sensitive zone and now he's managing to give me details about his life. Because your dad is not someone who talks to just anyone . . . On earth, he must have been very kind, but he must have had some sort of barrier up, and you couldn't enter into his bubble just like that."

This is true, and the same phrase, "into his bubble," is coming up for the third time.

"He has rejoined your brother. But there's still this second man, and the notion of a brother is very important, it was important for him to find him."

This brother again? This insistence is disconcerting.

"When you're saying that you see them, can you see what they're doing?"

"I see them. Not the same way I see you, because you are material and real, but I can sense their presence. I know where they are in the room. I see them in my head."

"But what about the photo? After I took it out, you only looked at it for thirty seconds and you haven't looked at it since. So how does it help?"

"It helps put me onto his vibration."

"Can you ask him what it was like for him after he died?"

"It was complicated. He had a hard time letting go. There were things he needed to say. His departure was . . . as if he were closing his eyes and never came back. There were very few words at the end. This frustrated him, as if he hadn't been able to finish saying the things he wanted to. He does say, though, that he was definitely not alone. This helped him to accept his leaving, the fact that he was surrounded by other people like that. He says that someone was there when he left. A presence in the room, even before he left. This presence reassured him. He was not alone. In spite of everything he still had a hard time going up, but once he realized that what was important was no longer on earth but somewhere else, he let go. Many people were expecting him on the other side. He's talking about the anguish he felt at the moment he passed. That fear of final judgement, the side of him that's a little religious, fear of not knowing where he would land . . . He's talking about a wide path, that he was welcomed on a wide path."

I am very moved by this description. Yes, our exchanges were very reserved in his final weeks. We talked, but did we talk about the important things? How could we? My father was tremendously worried about what would happen to him the moment he died. The thought terrified him. At the end of his life, he must have learned how to live with this fear, and this was not an easy thing. His inability to sleep was especially linked to this enormous fear, that of leaving during the night and never waking up to the rising sun again.

"He wants to thank you for something you did after his departure that has to do with the accompanying of his soul. He's thanking you because he was relieved that it happened like that, as if it would stay in the family."

The last hours of my father's life are on a beautiful sunny Sunday in June. Papa has been unconscious since the night before. I've been alone with him for several hours. My mother has left to rest at the house, and my brother Simon will be back soon. It is 3:45 p.m. I notice that Papa's breathing is even weaker. Now, there are only tiny and very weak inhalations. I ask the nurses if I should call my mother to tell her to come back sooner than she had planned. They tell me yes, probably.

He's not moving, not even a little.

Once my mother and Simon have been informed, I kneel down in front of the bed, my face near my father's, which is so emaciated. His half-closed eyes will never reopen; he's already on his way.

His body still isn't moving.

Very delicately, I take his hand in mine. I let him know just before I do it so that the contact of my fingers on his skin, even though it's very gentle, doesn't surprise him. He is leaving his body. His stirrings become subtle and begin to drift away with his waning body. I don't want to bring him back to it with my gesture. Gentleness is what's needed. Calm, silence, and delicate movements.

My dad is leaving.

Then I talk to him, very softly. The moment has come, I tell him, he doesn't need to be afraid, people are waiting for him. His mother, his dad, his son. I'm certain of it. Even though a few days ago I had been asking myself what the best way to help in this moment would be, now the words come by themselves. I'm not thinking anymore. Everything is natural and spontaneous and happy.

I repeat that he shouldn't be afraid. I tell him that everything he will see and hear are just creations of his spirit; the only thing that counts is the light. I murmur that he is a kind man, a kind husband to my mother, and that everything is calm and gentle, there's nothing to be afraid of in the place he's slipping into.

Then an incredible energy reigns in the room. A beautiful energy. The moment is intense, fundamental. This moment is beautiful. I am happy to be here.

And I *know* where he is going.

In this moment it's not about my knowledge, or something I read in a book or somewhere else. It comes from deep inside me. My whole body is filled with this certainty, with this knowledge of what is happening. And it's extraordinary. This journey, this transition, is beautiful. This is not death, even though we are separating from each other now. Even though we are never going to see each other again, life doesn't stop. Everything is clear in this instant. Intense, true, and simple.

Life doesn't stop. Death does not exist.

We are in a moment of dissolution. My father's life is being transformed. It is metamorphosing by detaching itself from matter cell by cell. It is becoming light again.

My father is being reborn somewhere else.

I am penetrated by this energy. At times, waves of colossal emotion briefly shake me. I tell my father how happy and proud I am to have been his son. He gave me every essential thing that a father could give a child. He is a good man to whom I am saying goodbye. And I will accompany him with these words that are coming out by themselves and that I'm repeating over and over. I tell him I love him, that everything is calm, serene, tranquil. I talk to him in a quiet voice. I am extremely careful not to offer any negative word, vigilant about my tone and that my choice of expressions is as appropriate as possible, the most peaceful and soothing it can be.

I talk to him endlessly about the light that he must already be seeing.

During this hour I have the physical feeling that he is diving into a whirlwind of emotions and energy, and that in this maelstrom only the light will be able to stabilize his spirit. I continue reminding him of this. I invite him to spot this light, then to slide toward it, dive into it, and let himself be surrounded by it. To let himself float in the light. I repeat this over and over.

My mother arrives and comes into the room. She takes my place next to Papa and I sit across from her. I am going to continue talking to him, to guide him intermittently, in the moments when my mother is not speaking to him herself. Then my father's breathing becomes weaker and weaker. Then his final movements, little twitches on the skin of his neck, cease.

There will be no great exhale, no sudden movement, no noise . . . just breathing that becomes so thin that it stops before we can really be sure. His muscles have not relaxed; he isn't showing any sign of finality. I place my glasses in front of his mouth to see if a light breath fogs the glass. Nothing. I take his pulse and it is then I realize that his heart is no longer beating.

An imperceptible death, so discreet.

At that very moment, Simon arrives in the room. All three of us are with Papa.

What has just happened? Why was life here, and why did it stop in the next moment? It really is a great mystery to observe. A mystery that is awe-inspiring.

We stay in the room, all three of us around his abandoned corpse. As he left, life has frozen this body in silence. The cold starts to extend over his face, which is now relaxed. He becomes pale. Life has left to go somewhere else.

It is Father's Day.

When we reflect seriously on the study of this subject, as I have been doing as a journalist for years, we discover rather quickly that the idea that life continues after death is a scientifically valid hypothesis. Dr. Jean-Jacques Charbonier, in particular, has been skillfully defending this observation for a long time. Knowing about Christelle's experiments with people in comas, he invited her to put her abilities to a scientific test.

Jean-Jacques Charbonier is an anesthetist in Toulouse who is a recognized specialist in near-death experiences, the famous NDE. He is also the author of numerous books on the subject.[9] For years, this physician has described how much these unexplained experiences with death, among which he places NDE at the top of the list, are objective elements that demonstrate that the consciousness—our soul, our spirit—cannot be reduced to the activity of our brains.

In other words, our spirit exists independently of our body, in such a way that when the brain dies, the consciousness does not disappear; it does not die.

We are not talking about the rantings of a lone physician here, but about a scientific hypothesis that today is garnering a large consensus in the medical community and around the world. In fact, the unprecedented accumulation of studies and testimonies[10]—ranging from NDE[11] to spontaneous contact with the deceased, from experiments of controlled mediumship to research on the conscious mind—makes the materialist vision (claiming that death is the end of all consciousness) henceforth scientifically untenable.

Let's repeat this: the idea that death does not exist is now a scientifically solid hypothesis.

Through his own means, Dr. Jean-Jacques Charbonier is taking part in this surge of worldwide research. The

---

9 Jean-Jacques Charbonier, *Les Sept Bonnes Raisons de croire à l'au-delà*, J'ai Lu, 2014; *La Médecine face à l'au-delà*, Trédaniel, 2010.
10 Stéphane Allix and Paul Bernstein (eds.), *Expériences extraordinaires. Le manuel clinique*, Dunod/InterEditions, 2013.
11 Pim van Lommel, *Consciousness Beyond Life: The Science of the Near-Death Experience*, HarperOne, 2010.

experiment with Christelle consists of testing what nursing staff and physicians sometimes experience in an intuitive way: the feeling of being able to communicate with patients in a coma or under general anesthesia. Christelle is very confident in the idea of this collaboration because she experiences this daily. But strangely, the experiment will prove to be demanding for her. Christelle will come out of it completely exhausted by a day that required much more energy than communicating with the deceased usually requires from her. The comatose patients drain her the most, more than the two people under general anesthesia she was successfully in contact with that morning.

Christelle knows nothing about the patient Jean-Jacques directs her to, except that he is a man who has been in a coma for a little over a week and who should be waking up, since he is no longer under any sedatives. But he is not.

When she enters the intensive care unit, Christelle has a small moment of hesitation. Usually in this medical universe she is a nurse's aide, and for a few seconds she has a hard time getting situated. Then she makes out the patient's soul in the process of . . . pacing, obviously annoyed and angry. This perception resituates Christelle in her role as medium. Jean-Jacques leaves her alone in the unit without a medical file or any information.

From the instant that Christelle takes the hand of the man in the coma, everything starts coming. The man tells her that he came to the ICU after "something went wrong with his stomach." He then explains that he drinks a lot, he smokes, and that he doesn't place much of a priority on his health because he's depressed and "couldn't care less." His level of discontent is obvious, and he has one hell of a personality. He gives his age, then several other details about his illness, as well as his life and family. Everything comes in fits and starts, but very precisely. At the end he reveals to her that at the moment he is having a stroke.

Ten minutes later, Jean-Jacques returns to the unit and Christelle tells him everything, most importantly the fact that the patient is having a stroke. The doctor examines the patient's pupils and notices that there does indeed seem to be a small neurological issue. Jean-Jacques reassures Christelle. In this situation, there is nothing abnormal about this. Impressed, he confirms the truth of the other medical information she provided to him. The "thing that went wrong in the stomach" is translated in medical terms as "aortic rupture" in the stomach, which would indeed indicate "something going wrong." As it turns out, all the perceptions of a medical nature are able to be validated by Jean-Jacques immediately by looking at the file in his hand. He is astounded. As far as the information about his family relationships, the doctor will have to investigate by talking to the patient's sister. She will confirm, among other things, that her brother has an obnoxious personality and leads a riotous life.

This experience proves, if there were ever any need for it, that people in a deep coma can hear us and are aware of what is happening around them, even though their body and brain are not reactive.

Christelle doesn't usually push her dialogues with comatose people this far. When she is working, she tries to close herself off to avoid feeling too much empathy, because this would affect her tasks as a nurse's aide. This experience in Toulouse was her first time doing this. In her practice, contact is made more through intuition or flashes that advise her to make certain movements when she is near a patient in a coma or in the intensive care unit.

She is not the only person who has experienced this. In fact, without being mediums, a number of people experience these moments of intuition, caregivers and parents alike: we have the feeling of taking the person's hand; something *pushes* us to make this kind of gesture. Is it the person in the coma who is expressing themself? We know intuitively what has to be done. This remark by Christelle resonates with me after the experience I had accompanying my father.

In these kinds of contexts, people even claim to have heard a voice speaking to them. This was not the case for me, but it has happened to Dr. Charbonier, when an intubated patient in a coma informed him that she was suffocating. Her voice echoed in the doctor's head, and instead of not paying attention to it, he decided to listen. After checking, he saved her life: she was indeed suffocating.

In addition to these feelings of intuition, Christelle also has the ability to see the soul of a comatose person. The patient is lying in bed and she sees a milky silhouette next to the body, or overhead, or even farther away from the physical body; strolling in the hospital hallway, for example. In that case, Christelle observes the silver cord that joins this silhouette to the physical body. It is very visible to her and its energy can be felt. To her, this is the most obvious sign that there is still life and hope that the soul may rejoin the body. The soul appears in the form of a whitish silhouette, a little opaque. Unlike the deceased, Christelle does not see clothing when she is in contact with the soul of a person in a coma, just a silhouette. And if the comatose person is in a state of distress, if for example they are undergoing a kind of medical intervention even though there is no longer a possibility of bringing them back to life, the soul is grayish, and this is the sign that it is time to let the person leave, in Christelle's eyes. A grayish soul, she explains, wants to go up, to leave. It's over. A whitish soul, slightly opaque, on the other hand, is synonymous with life, and is a sign that the person can come back.

In one intensive care unit where she works part of the night, Christelle has witnessed phenomena, to say the least. Every night, the faucets with photoelectric cells would switch on by themselves. These were faucets that had to have a hand passed under them to get the water to run. Now they were turning on by themselves, even though nobody was putting their hands underneath. No one of flesh and bone, anyway. Christelle observed that the soul of one of the hospitalized patients was taking a little stroll and playing with the taps. The soul of another comatose woman used to like pulling the nurses' hair when they were on break.

Contrary to the idea that hospitals are filled with wandering souls in suffering, Christelle's personal experiences give her more of a feeling that a good number of the comatose are walking around amusing themselves. Seeing those milky shapes still linked by a kind of silver umbilical cord is what allows her to tell the difference between these souls and the deceased. If there is a thread, it's a coma, if there is no longer a thread, the soul is in another world.

But the comatose are not always content with these small promenades through the hospital. Christelle reveals that certain souls enter immaterial spheres, while others never quite leave the intensive care unit. These latter ones are constantly making demands on living people, trying to communicate with them and sending signs.

A person can in fact be very confused while in a coma. They may experience different types of mental states, ranging from extreme confusion to the clearest awareness. Some understand easily what is happening, while others encounter the deceased, and still others undergo the evanescence of this mental state. But in every case, the medium reminds us, they are accompanied, they are not alone. The deceased, their guides, are watching over them.

As we continue the séance, my father begins talking about his funeral.

"There was not a normal ceremony?" Christelle asks me.

"Ask him to describe it."

"It's not a normal ceremony. Something a little bit unique was done, he's talking about takeoff, as if people helped him take off . . . There were bird songs outside, as if nature was on alert. He was very sensitive to all of this."

My mother, Simon, and I organized his funeral. We all wanted it to be held at the house. My father's casket was placed outside on a rug, and all of the family and friends that were present took their places outside on the terrace in front of his studio. The clouds had been worrying us since the morning, but the sun appeared and made the birds sing throughout the whole ceremony.

"He's showing me how he is dressed in the casket . . . He said he looked handsome, that your mother had done everything she could to make him handsome. This allowed him to reconcile with his body, that was important. He didn't like his body at the end of his life. He's thanking your mom for what she gave him because she invested her body and soul and it meant so much to him. 'I would like to thank her infinitely for this gesture of love that she knew how to give me,' he's saying. He's also talking about the ring. Again, he'd like to thank her for leaving it with him. But he's showing me that at one time people wanted her to take it back and then it was left with him later."

My mother wanted my father to buried with his ring. She put it on his finger when we dressed him together for the burial. In the end I advised my mother to take it off his finger and not to put it back on until the last moment. This is what she did.

"He's saying, 'Thank you, it was better that way.' He's adding that his things were saved, but that one object in

particular had been left and that this was important to him
. . . He's talking about . . . oh, about when he was inside his
'box.' 'Tell them I love them with all my heart. That even if
sometimes I wasn't able to be everything they expected me
to be, tell them that I'm doing well and that I love them infinitely.'"

I notice that Papa started by mentioning his casket and
something important that was left inside. This came completely from him, without any prompting.

"He's fixated on one thing he left on earth, something
that needs to be continued or perpetuated. It's something
tangible, it's troubling him, is there a question you want to
ask him?"

What does he want to talk about? My father had written
a short book about what painting represented for him. He
had put me in charge of publishing it, which I am still in the
process of doing. Is that what this is about? Or the objects
from the test?

"What is this tangible thing?" I ask Christelle.

"It's an object . . . no, objects. There are several of them,
it has to do with something he did a lot of when he was alive.
An activity he did all the time, a drawing or something like
that. He's showing me pieces of chalk . . . He's bursting out
laughing. He's saying, 'I know that it's tangible but that's all
you're asking for.' As if he were supposed to give you material things. He's talking about something that's expected,
an answer that's being expected . . . I don't know, he's saying he's doing his best, that he hears everything you're telling
him. He's laughing because he says sometimes there's nothing
he can do . . . He's telling me, 'Sometimes he's frustrated,'
meaning you. Because there are things you're waiting for with
much anticipation, and he can't necessarily give them to you.

Not everything comes that way, it's much more complicated in the beyond."

I'm stunned. At this point, Christelle doesn't know that I'm waiting for a specific piece of information from my father. But if he manages to say all of this, why doesn't he just give a list of the objects? "Not everything comes that way, it's much more complicated in the beyond." I have no doubt. But if he is capable of saying that, then he is more than capable of also giving me a list, no? This is incomprehensible.

"He's telling you, 'Don't give up.' I have the impression that he's rushing, like he doesn't have enough time . . . He's saying things quickly . . . He is still very fixated on material things. You asked him for material things? He needs to show those things, he's showing me several images, several things."

"Describe those images to me."

Having accompanied so many people, Christelle has become very familiar with the moment when a person leaves their present existence. Her double experience as both a caregiver and a medium has given her a rather complete expertise.

At the end of life, the dying person puts themselves in a sort of bubble, the energy changes, and any person who comes near will penetrate this bubble. In addition, this should not be done without letting the person know, because we are entering the dying person's privacy and this could be a bad experience for them. Even if, and especially if, the person is unconscious. They must be warned about each thing we are doing to them: if we are leaving the room, if we are staying in the room. And if we touch them, it is very important to let them know beforehand, whether it be to care for them or even simply for a caress: "I'm going to touch you, I'm putting my hand on your arm."

Certain dying people might be bothered by leaving in the presence of their loved ones. They would rather die alone. This is their own moment, it's private, and sometimes they do not wish to share it. Perhaps this is because they want to protect us, too, protect their family, since the end of life can be rather striking on a physical level: breathing is jagged, the cheeks become hollow, and the eyes, if not already closed, cloud over.

As a general rule, in the final minutes, when the passing is so close to beginning, Christelle observes a total relaxation, regardless of what their concerns or fears had been. And don't the dying probably see for several days what lies ahead of them? How many times has Christelle seen patients nearing the end of their life staring directly at one point in their room? Their gaze seems fixed on the void. But in reality they are often seeing the light, or their deceased loved ones. Christelle recently had a case where an old man saw his wife come sit down in the armchair next to his bed. She had died six months before him. This reassured him, even if he didn't really understand why she was coming. He didn't realize that she had come to get him. She was just there.

Christelle uses an expression to summarize what she observes at the moment of the death. She talks about a "continuity of the soul." She recognizes that observing this, to literally see that life does not stop, helps her a great deal in her work. In fact, because she is such an empathetic person, if she did not also have her medium side, she is not at all certain that she would continue in her medical profession, which can be so trying. Seeing this continuity of the soul, being a witness to everything that falls into place during death—the moving energies, the deceased who are becoming active on the other side, the guides, that whole celestial universe coming to life to welcome the person who is passing—all of this also gives death another dimension.

Christelle feels when the atmosphere in a room changes and when death is near. The vibrations change. It's unexplained today, but this hasn't prevented a number of Christelle's nursing colleagues from noticing it, too. This might manifest itself as goosebumps, for example. We might also have the feeling of being rocked, finding ourselves in something wrapping around us, a new energy, or other signs of a vibratory change that affect the room. Then the soul begins the process of detachment, and the energy level rises. At that moment, people in the room might burst into tears. The intensity of the moment probably explains this sudden fit of emotion, of course, but it could also be the effect of the ambient energy's transformation on the body.

I can attest to this myself. While I was talking to my father at least an hour before his departure, I was suddenly seized by a discharge of emotion and started sobbing. But it was not out of grief, pain, or sadness. It was an intensity that *physically* shook me, like a wave, intense and powerful. Pure energy.

Christelle says that this happens when the celestial energies mix with earthly energies. A sort of vortex opens up. A passage, a tunnel, descends into the room, a tunnel through which different energies are passing to act as guides for the deceased. They make trips back and forth when they are not waiting in the room. Once, Christelle came into a room and stumbled upon ten people from the celestial world waiting for their loved one, who was in the process of slipping away in his bed.

This passage, this airlock, this tunnel, has a physical presence.

Christelle sees it, whether death takes place at the hospital or after a brutal or accidental end to the person's life, all the time.

After death, in whatever manner the person left (illness, accident, etc.), the first hours that follow are critical. What has just happened to the soul is overwhelming. In a way, the soul is still tied to its earthly body, even if this body no longer serves any purpose.

The soul needs to be in a certain form of serenity. And the way that the earthly envelope is treated counts. This is why Christelle places so much importance on the mortuary cleaning. During those first hours in the beyond, the soul must understand where it is. It has just moved from one world to another.

Talking to the soul helps a lot.

Christelle reminds us that in France, nothing forbids a member of the family from asking to perform the mortuary cleaning themselves. The law allows this. Nurses may react by refusing, but know that they are committing an abuse of authority if they do this, and that you have the law behind you. Their role is to make sure that you are psychologically capable of doing it, not to arbitrarily deny you your right.

This goes for both the hospital and the funeral home. On their end, the funeral home may also be opposed and present you with all kinds of arguments to try to dissuade you, because involving the family represents another responsibility and, just like at the hospital, they don't want to have to deal with those kinds of things.

Christelle nevertheless insists: in order to keep this moment from being more difficult than it already is by adding the guilt of not feeling capable of taking care of all of this, it is still possible to very effectively accompany one's deceased loved one simply by speaking to them. It's important to keep this in mind and not to think that the passage of the loved one will be impossible because the room needs to be emptied quickly and the body must be sent directly to the cold room. Whether out loud or in our heads, we can speak to them and they will hear us. It's a good idea to tell them what's happening, to remind them that they will be fine where they are going. Encourage them to free themselves.

Christelle explains that on the other side, different vibratory levels and spheres are waiting for them. The new arrivals pass through a sort of regenerative sphere where they regain their energy. Beyond that, she does not venture into too many suppositions. Whatever ideas and intuitions we may have, our suppositions and earthly feelings can only go so far.

The other side is a much subtler world.

There we find this hierarchy of vibratory levels. We talk about the "source." There are people who surround the source, those who are far away from it. The source? Maybe it's the famous light that so many have seen when they experienced being on the border between life and death.

The séance is coming to a close. My father managed to spontaneously tell Christelle that he knows what I'm expecting from him. He's doing his best, he adds, but it doesn't seem to be very easy for him. Interesting. But why is it difficult? Why doesn't he simply say the names of the objects that I hid in the casket? Christelle says he's speaking quickly, that he's showing her material things, many images . . .

"Describe these images to me."

"It's mainly small wooden boxes that have all kinds of things inside . . . long, sliding things. Things ranging from pencils, a lot of chalk, pastels, lots of colored things. He's also showing . . . something with a hat . . . an old map. These objects were very valuable to him. He's showing me many objects."

"Tell me what objects he's showing you."

"Outside of that, a large bookshelf, books, encyclopedias, books talking about the world. He's also showing me his desk, his little corner. There are more things that belong to him, his papers . . . He says it's normal: 'It's normal, all this paper, it's normal . . .' and he's showing me the casket . . . Oh, I don't like this."

"What?"

"I don't like when they show me the caskets . . . It's making him laugh, but not me."

This is making Papa laugh, but me less so. I feel that he is here. That he's turning around us, that he's not able to capture Christelle's spirit adequately. She gives me the impression that she has been invaded by images that she's no longer able to sort through.

"Don't censor yourself," I tell her. "Describe all of the images that come to you."

"He's showing me something made of wood that was put in the casket, something very important and that is a part of him. It's not in a photo, but it's a very tangible thing. There are lots of wooden boxes. A ton of them, so that he can organize his things. Lots of little things, looks like chalk, tubes, there are a lot of pastels, pastel colors . . . He's getting angry, he's not happy. I can't tell what he wants."

This is unbelievable! It's so clear to me: I am witnessing my father's efforts to transmit the details of those objects. Let's summarize: he explained to Christelle that I'm expecting information about objects that were placed in his casket, that these objects are his life. He gave birth to an image of a little box with a range of colors inside. He's talking about a "tube" of color. He also mentioned the books, "books talking about the world." I have the irritating feeling that I am playing charades. Except here, the one who is miming has been dead for over a year. And according to Christelle, even he is starting to get annoyed.

"I'm going back . . . He's talking about the fabric in his casket. He says, 'The fabric.' Okay . . . there's something with his shoes, um . . . oh, okay, he's showing details, it doesn't really matter."

But it does *matter!* I can't help thinking.

"He's showing me a lot of things inside his casket. There's white, white fabric, he's focused on the fabric, he's showing me a lot of images."

"What are these images?"

"White fabric . . . actually, there's something by his feet that I can't make out, I have a lot of white fabric. As if it were covered in fabric . . . I don't want to think too much when I'm not receiving clearly . . . I'm going to stop because otherwise it just becomes me stitching things together. I can't see it, but I feel like it's important to him, the inside of the casket. Well, he's calling it the 'box.'"

I remind you that the objects were under the white fabric that covered my father's body. To be certain that no one would see them by accident, I put them against his legs, far beneath the white fabric.

What is happening here is fascinating. But something is not getting through. For the first time, Christelle realizes that it may have to do with her. Either way, something is not getting through. Well, that's not entirely true, lots of things are getting through: his illness, his headache, his personality, his insistency, his annoyance. She is with my father. She is capturing his intentions, but she is visibly affected by his urging. Yes, what's inside the casket is important. Christelle understands this: "I can tell he wants to go into greater detail." Under the white fabric, near his feet . . . How can I relax her? It's almost infuriating to be so close to what I'm looking for.

"Do you feel him here? Is he present?"

"Yes, he's here, but he's kind of doing a zigzag. Your brother is here, too."

"Can we go back to the images you had before?"

"There are images, sensations, one object in particular is important, something having to do with the family. But as

113

soon as I want to go deeper, the fact that I'm afraid is blocking me, I'm thinking too much and I can't see anything. I'm
very stressed as soon as I start thinking too much. I know this
is getting us stuck, and that it's bothering him. He's grumbling and suddenly I end up sabotaging myself . . . He can't
stand it."

"Well, what I'm asking him to tell me about is what I put
in his casket."

"Oh jeez . . ."

"But what did he show you?"

"A box, something made of wood. Something long and
thin . . . not a stick, like a stick but smaller."

Something long and thin, like a stick but smaller. A paintbrush? Christelle doesn't say this but no one could have described it better.

"I can't do it, you've fixated me on it."

"Didn't I need to?"

"The problem is that when I fixate on it, I think too
much."

"I thought it would help you concentrate."

"No."

"I thought it would relax you."

"No. I definitely realized that there was a story about the
casket since he was showing it to me. Your father knows the
code, but I'm the one who's not able to see it."

"But why isn't he able to talk to you, to simply say something to you, like 'caramel,' for example?"

"Because it's not that easy."

"Why isn't it that easy?"

"I don't know."

"And why don't you know?"

"Has anyone ever told you how annoying you are?" She
laughs. "This happens often in a séance. And what about

your part of the job? Maybe those on the other side need *us* to make progress, to reflect."

"Yes, but in this situation, I'm not waiting for advice about my personal life . . . I have a deal with him."

"I know there's a deal because he's coming back to it, but you're the one who has given him this mission. Is it really his mission, too, on the other side?"

"I know him, he's my father."

"True, ever since a little while ago he hasn't stopped showing me this image. I know this is making him angry because he'd really like this to get through."

"The difficulty is coming from the communication between the two of you?"

"Yes, it's not easy for them to come down and transmit messages, just like it's not easy for us as mediums to climb up in vibration high enough to reach them. So sometimes they have to descend even further, if we're tired, for example. Lots of things can take a toll."

"Sure, should we stop here?"

"Yes, let's stop . . . The colors are really great, it's impressive; I've never seen so many colors before."

"Is he still here?"

"Yes."

"How can you sense his presence?"

"I know he's here."

"On your right?"

"Yes. I feel him and as soon as I want to see him, I see him. But as soon as I don't want to see him anymore, I won't see anything at all. I've learned to focus."

"But is he waiting?"

"Yes, he's waiting, they're waiting. They're the ones who decide how much time they need to spend with us."

"And now he's not saying anything?"

"No, he's waiting. His hands behind his back."

"Okay . . . so should we tell him goodbye?"

"Yes, but he's going to stay . . . How long ago did he leave?"

"A year and a half."

"That's what I thought. A new energy."

"Does that have anything to do with the fact that he's having trouble expressing things?"

"It could, yes. It's possible that his vibration isn't strong enough for me to understand, and since I'm a little tired it's hard for me to climb up toward him. Time can play a role, yes. A year and a half, that's just yesterday in celestial time."

I am shaken.

I feel like I just played Pictionary with the afterlife. For a whole hour, my father drew many things in Christelle's spirit to lead her to understand that the objects were hidden in his casket, and to try to show her what the objects were. What has just happened in this séance is rich with important things to remember. To me, the test is conclusive, even if it was not officially a success.

But what is most dear to me is the extraordinary bond I see at work between me and my father. It has survived death.

Pierre

Pierre Yonas lives on a small street in southern Paris. As I do before each meeting with a medium, I speak to my father out loud. The neighborhood is deserted at this hour of the morning. As I walk, I ask him again to be kind enough to make an effort to tell the medium what is hidden in the casket. I don't know how he will take it, what this means for him, but I have realized that it is not as simple as I thought, even if I can't quite figure out why.

In fact, I don't know *where* my father is.

I don't know if time has taken its toll, if he is still the same person as the one I knew. I don't know what he does, what he looks like, or what the world he lives in looks like.

In fact, I don't know anything. Except the fact that he is *alive.*

Which is already pretty good, I'd say. I know there is a form of life after death. But beyond this observation, I am noticing that my questions have become even greater in number than before. And death remains foreign to me behind the immense wall of fog.

As I approach Pierre's place I list out loud, one more time, the objects I placed with my father. I add, insistently, that if he is not capable of giving me the names of all of the objects, I would like him to try to talk about the book, *The*

Tartar Steppe, and the compass—I know, not the easiest ones to choose.

I met Pierre years ago, during the filming of *Extraordinary Investigations*,[12] the documentary series I was presenting on channel M6. Pierre is a medium, but he is also a healer and a seer, three activities that he manages with ease and vigor. I am very confident because I know his abilities, but at the same time I can't help but be worried. In my recent meetings I have seen just how much the emotional parameters, such as a medium's stress level, can interfere with a séance, never mind other, even more mysterious factors.

No, communicating with the dead is not so simple. I really hope that Pierre and my father are going to be able to make it happen.

Pierre was a foster child. His mother, a young woman not even of age, full of dreams and in love with freedom, had been seduced by an American soldier stationed in France. She got pregnant, but the soldier returned to his country at the end of his service. Twenty-six days after his birth, Pierre was abandoned by this very young mother who felt incapable of taking on the responsibility of motherhood by herself.

But Pierre has never had abandonment issues. This man feels things deeply. For him it's a physical sensation, and he has always had the profound intuition that he chose to incarnate himself, chose his mother, and whispered his first name in her ear. He also knew where his life would go. There is no bitterness about that, no resentment. He always went for-

---

12 *Enquêtes extraordinaires*, seasons 1 and 2, *Les Signes de l'au-delà*, and *Ils communiquent avec les morts*, documentaries directed by Natacha Calestrémé et al., DVD, Éd. Montparnasse, 2011 and 2014.

ward, with a tremendous force of character. Pierre is a solid man, in the proper and figurative senses of the phrase. He is built like an athlete, with wide shoulders. Complain? No, never. The abandonment issue is what others project onto him. "I decided to be here, I chose that mom who would disappear and who I'd find again."

Today he is forty-nine years old.

Placed very early on with a foster family, this child's behavior and comments are *different*. "He has a boo-boo there," he says in front of a perfect stranger, pointing his finger at part of the man's body. This is astonishing when we discover that the man in question revealed that he did have a health problem in the area the little boy had pointed to. If this had happened once, it could have been a coincidence, but after several times the people around him quickly become uncomfortable.

Visions are added to these stupendous intuitions. This proves to be a constant in the childhood of mediums. Pierre remembers that when people would visit his adoptive parents, like the friends of his father who came to play cards on Sundays, he would see the friends but also a lady, a child, or sometimes a grandfather enter with them. He would see them like he saw the others, but he noticed that during the whole time they were there, no one spoke one word to them, and he couldn't understand this.

At this time, nothing interferes with what he's sensing. Pierre is a child, a pure creature with one foot in the beyond and one foot here. So he sees dead people. This is why no one speaks to them: the others don't see them.

Today Pierre practices three activities that, for him, are inseparable from one another: healer, seer, and medium. Many of the people he cares for are children. A number of them confide in him and admit, for example, that they have seen a man in their bedroom, or a deceased grandmother. These kinds of perceptions, like those of his own childhood, are not that exceptional, he recognizes. To a greater or lesser degree, we all had access as children. Accepting these perceptions from a young age allows them to develop more easily. Acceptance favors a purer connection.

But fear is often a hindrance to this acceptance, our own fear and the fear of those around us, like our parents. When he is little, Pierre finds himself alone in the face of this invisible world. It is terrifying at first because these appearances happen when he is not expecting them: at night, during the day, any time. He deals with them. One of his most frightening memories is probably his discovery that no one else but him sees what he sees. "Why? What's the matter with me?"

This is revealed by the sudden vision he has of a deceased person while he is sitting on the bench during a basketball game. Or, hidden under the sheets, he may feel a presence, open one eye, and find himself face to face with an old lady or man who does not live in his house. Another time, he is at the house of a friend whose grandfather lives in the countryside and keeps horses. While he is outside, Pierre sees a girl riding a horse in the distance. But the closer she gets, the more transparent she becomes, and when she reaches him, there's only the horse, with no one on it. When he shares what he has just seen and describes the young girl to the grandfather, the man goes completely white and exclaims, "That's my sister who died sixty years ago!"

Pierre lives his childhood and the beginning of adolescence with the feeling that he is being constantly watched, as if he is never alone, not even for one moment. Being unable to confide in anyone is a terrible burden. How can he talk about this to his adoptive parents, Catholics who don't believe in spirits? Even though they live in a rural area where these things are often accepted, the subject is not part of their universe.

So Pierre stays quiet and copes with it.

Like Henry Vignaud, he will not receive any explanations about what he is experiencing until adolescence, during an encounter with a being of light.

A meeting that will change everything.

There is an enormous difference between the soul of a deceased person and that of a being of light who is not incarnated: as much as the first can be worrying, in the presence of the light, Pierre feels confident and instantly at peace. Everything releases. His fear disappears.

He is sixteen at the time. He is on vacation in Martigues, in the south, at his adoptive sister's house. He is lying on his bed when something wakes him up. He opens his eyes and suddenly sees in front of him a being that seems to fill the entire room with how impressive he is. Pierre can no longer move. The being is gigantic, probably six and a half feet tall. Pierre remembers that he was completely awake. When he opens his eyes, he turns his head, and that is when he sees this entity. From the instant he sees it, Pierre is no longer able to move his head or body. What is standing before him has the appearance of a human body, but he can't make out a face. The hands are not visible, either. The being is a blazing white that for some reason does not blind Pierre.

What happens next is astounding.

The being comes closer. Pierre notices that his arms end in abnormally long fingers, like points. It looks like a body made of energy, and the ends of its arms look sharpened. These extremities have a golden color while the rest of the being is very white. He comes closer, lifts his arms, and places his extremities on Pierre's body, as an acupuncturist would do. He stops this way at several different points along Pierre's body. Pierre expects to feel the pricking but, on the contrary, he is surprised to feel no pain. What the being of light is doing sometimes even causes very pleasant sensations.

Pierre is paralyzed and in a state of indescribable lethargy. His emotions are intensified. Unable to move, he is almost in a state of shock and, at the same time, confident and relaxed. Reflexively, while the tension he feels allows him to very slowly move again, he tries to push the being away with his foot. His numb leg takes an unbelievably long time to react. Then he is able to lift it and touch the entity. He feels a shock, a resistance, and almost simultaneously the being disappears, crossing through the wall of the room with a piercing noise.

The noise wakes up Pierre's sister and her husband. They chalk it up to a nightmare.

What has just happened to him? Having faced his experiences alone ever since he was a child, Pierre's reaction has been to progressively distance himself from his perceptions. They are too uncontrollable, too invasive. He does not want to accept what he is experiencing. He does not want to be a medium, to possess those tools, that knowledge, those abilities.

The being of light has come to reactivate them.

Pierre explains today that recognizing his abilities was like accepting a mission, that of opening a door to the deceased. And he is guided in this direction.

At the age of twenty-three, he decides to abandon the athletic career he had chosen and begins his work as a healer. Mediumship establishes itself in parallel as he continues to see the deceased next to his patients. To him, mediumship calls on the same energy as the one he uses as a healer.

But what exactly do we mean by energy?

Pierre receives people in the small apartment he lives in on the ground floor, two welcoming rooms in the image of the man who invites me in, joking. He seems relaxed. So much the better. Like the others, Pierre does not know anything about the nature of the test. Even if all of the mediums I meet suspect that I'm not just asking them to do this séance for no reason, they think they are participating in a simple consultation intended to illustrate the way they work, and that the interview will be the larger piece of our discussion. At this point, I am not using the word "test" with them.

Sitting on the couch in the living room, I place the photo of my father on the coffee table, indicating only that this is the man I would like to communicate with. Pierre takes the photo, holds it in his hands, and passes his thumb over my father's face.

"This departure seems recent to me. Very recent, about two years?"

"Yes."

"He's talking to me about his respiratory problem, feeling suffocated. My lungs are being compressed. The thoracic cage being blocked, does that make sense?"

"Yes."

"And he's walking slowly. As if someone is holding onto him, he's trembling."

"Yes."

"These respiratory problems . . . I'm getting emphysema, I have that when I'm thinking about him, is that the case?"

"Yes."

Pierre has instantly connected, it seems. The cardiac failure my father suffered from for years had actually provoked the problem with his lungs: emphysema. It was from the moment the emphysema was diagnosed that his health started to deteriorate.

"This man has a lot of personality."

"Yes."

"A lot of personality, but a lot of silence, too, someone who knew when not to say anything . . . These are energies that both of you share. Is he part of your family?"

"Yes."

"Seeing all of the books he has is funny. Lots of books . . . history, always about history. He's always into history; this man is unusual."

"Yes?"

"Very into history, he loves history. One period in particular, we could say . . . a father . . . is it your father?"

"Yes."

"There's someone around him who liked military things a lot?"

"In what way?"

"A military history, in his family . . . army, military . . . not him but in the family."

"Yes."

"There's a military side to him, something about the army. His story is very close to the family, anyway."

"Yes."

My father's grandfather was the son of a polytechnic graduate and was also one himself. He left the army, where he served with an engineering company, with the rank of captain. Several of my father's uncles were also in the military. That's without counting those who were called to serve during the First World War like his own father, Louis, who was wounded in the foot. Apart from that, the keen interest in history that my father nurtured led him to become fascinated with great military figures and tumultuous periods in our past. He considered *War and Peace* the greatest book ever written; without exaggerating, he must have read it forty times.

"He's a man with principles, very cultured, a very rooted upbringing . . . as if he had survived something significant that allows him to have these values about life . . . sometimes too many, perhaps . . . did he have trouble walking?"

"Can he be more specific?"

"It's like he had something wrong with one of his legs."

"When?"

"Late in life."

"Yes."

My father's deteriorating state of health caused his legs to bother him. Near the end, my brother and I had to help him when he wanted to walk.

"Like he's leaning, hunched over . . . a great fatigue."

"Yes."

"He's talking to me about a story with trains. Railroad lines, trains, movements . . ."

"That's vague."

"Yes, but there are a lot of people returning in the trains. He's a spectator . . . This affected him; he's little. It's like he experienced the war."

"That's the case, yes."

"He saw terrible things . . . He kept quiet about it. He didn't talk about it with you. 'There was no point,' he's telling me."

"He's telling you that?"

"Yes . . . 'There was no point.' He's not the kind of person to stir things up . . . The past is the past. He was very young."

This brings one episode to mind. I can't remember how the subject came up in the conversation, but when the two of us were alone, my father talked to me about the only time he had refused to shake a man's hand. Two men, as it happened. It had to do with two former members of the SS, years after the war, who were in business with one of his acquaintances. When he learned about their past, he had refused to greet them. This gesture seemed to assume so much importance to him, though he was usually someone who was so accommodating. My father very rarely allowed himself to be won over by emotion, but as he talked about this he had tears in his eyes. He confided a few scraps of his memories of the Occupation to me, and the image that had given birth to such hatred toward those two SS members, the image of the men and women who had been deported. "Even children, can you imagine?" Then he stopped talking, too emotional to continue.

"There's a man with brown hair next to him, someone who disappeared as a young person. He's saying, 'Like a brother.' Did he lose a young brother?"

"I can't answer that."

"With brown hair."

"I can't say."

"He's repeating, 'Like a brother.'"

"Can he give me more specific details?"

"I have a guy named Charlot, something like that. Charles, that doesn't mean anything to you?"

"No."

"You're going to look for him . . . As if he was a hidden brother. I'm being told about a secret, something hidden."

"I have no idea."

Without saying anything to Pierre, I feel disconcerted. Here for a second time is the apparition of this "hidden brother" with the same name that Christelle Dubois gave me: Charles. I had spoken about it with my mother; it didn't mean anything to her. My father must have not known about it, either. I can't imagine that he would never have told us, or his wife, if he had known. It's a mystery. There is no longer anybody alive in the family who would be able to tell us more. What could be done? If my father had had a close friend whose name was Charles and who he might have considered like a brother, maybe, but he didn't have any friends named Charles. Not one. Could it be one of the babies my grandmother had lost in her miscarriages before my father? How could I know? Will I ever find out the truth about this story?

One observation drew Pierre's attention at a young age. Years were going by, and he realized that one detail that had seemed random to him in reality revealed an invariable rule.

The deceased people who showed themselves to him did not speak.

And those who spoke to him did not show themselves.

There has never been an exception. Of all the deceased who have appeared before him in a visible body, not one has ever spoken a word to him. He has seen them smiling or sad, but they remain tirelessly immobile and silent. What's more, these apparitions are those of people showing themselves on their best day. Pierre has never seen a wounded body, one covered in blood, or other horrific visions, regardless of the circumstances of the person's death. Here's one more thing we can leave for the movies. And those who remain invisible, like my father is at this moment, speak by slipping words into his mind, by showing images corresponding to their appearance, to the way they died, and a thousand other things. But they stay invisible.

For Pierre, this is tied to a question of energy. The energy the deceased use to show themselves, to create a body with which they can make themselves visually perceptible, must be so great that they don't have enough left to do anything but create this image in our world. On the other hand, those who speak don't have the energy or the strength needed to show themselves at the same time.

Everything is energy, everything is vibration.

Energy is the key that opens the gate to the spirit world and makes communication with the dead possible. In order to pass from the place they occupy to here—our material world, which must create a great deal of interference—they need energy. A lot of energy. Pierre uses the image of a voyage they make through a reality filled with many obstacles that they have to avoid: evil thoughts, other souls, electricity, telluric waves, etc. All of these material things that make up so many disruptive vibrations.

The same is true on Pierre's side. He also needs energy to make himself permeable to the messages from the deceased. For example, when he takes the photo of my father and holds it in his hand while passing his fingers over it, he says he is trying to put himself into a state of more basic energy, the most animal energy possible, so that he can change levels and put himself in a vibration that will transport him somewhere else. A photo is a light, subtle energy, a bridge.

When I observe Pierre, I can feel this animal energy overflowing from the edges of his body. I feel like he is ready to spring and I can easily imagine how rapidly this instinctive side can activate inside him.

The less he thinks, he says, the better he picks things up.

Reflection is the poison of feeling, and the more we ask questions, the more the sensation is concealed.

By taking the photo, he is suddenly creating a vacuum. He dives into a state in which he tries to be as empty and serene as possible. To do this, he forgets who he is, his personality, what he knows how to do, everything he has learned. He compares this state to an amnesia that can last a few seconds at the most. From then on, he begins having new physical sensations. It's a little as if he were here without being here. Then his consciousness transforms, and like an antenna, he feels that things are arriving in him. On the empty screen of his spirit, the imported details appear. Character traits emerge like foreign, unexpected pieces. These belong to the deceased person, who is entering into communication and is settling, very subtly, into Pierre's head. He then feels what the person was like. Their personality traits, unknown to Pierre, appear superimposed on his own. During the séance, he allows himself to be invaded little by little by another personality. This is not possession, even if it seems like it. Pierre describes this process more as "transfiguration." It is in this state that he hears sentences, picks up flashes, images, smells, or physical feelings.

The deceased are using Pierre's brain. It rubs off on him.

Two souls, in the space of a few fractions of a second, are in the same body. That's the secret.

This mechanism of impregnation is dependent upon the energy of the deceased, who must try to blend with Pierre to establish contact. This explains the precision of certain communications and the imprecision of others. This exercise takes practice on both sides. Much depends on the level of ease the conscious energy will be capable of. Pierre doesn't like to say that he speaks with the dead. What dead people? They are alive on the other side, so he prefers the term "conscious energy."

If the soul has poor control over this energy, or if it is not used to it because the death is too recent, a clear and precise synchronization will not be possible. The right balance needs to be found, the thinnest common thread. The shoddier the transfiguration, the more the zone of exchange—the space shared by the deceased and Pierre—will be shoddy, blurred, and the transmission will often lack precision. The communication will then be more of an approximation; the details given will be poorly defined. It is the medium's job at that time to share things, and this is when errors and incorrect interpretations slip in. Imagine a conversation between two people who had several handkerchiefs in front of their mouths.

Now we know: communicating with the dead does not appear to resemble an ordinary conversation. A kind of osmosis between the deceased and the medium to facilitate a sharing of knowledge, now that's a more accurate picture.

In a few moments, to my great surprise, Pierre will be the second medium to capture my father's uncle, Paul, who disappeared on the frontlines in 1915 in the middle of the month of February. Pierre is going to feel like it's very cold out, that it's wartime, and he will even have the feeling of being there. What's going to happen to him? The cold will surround Pierre in one fell swoop. This detail will be given by the spirit of Uncle Paul, mixed with Pierre's own spirit, to indicate the era that the deceased wants to pay attention to. The information passes physically to Pierre, who will put it into words. Paul puts himself in the moment of his death; the memory of the cold on his skin becomes more distinct and this sensation passes instantly to Pierre, whose own skin will shiver as if his epidermis belonged to Paul for the space of a second. Yes, two souls in one body.

But it goes further than this. Pierre can sense the spirits coming. He notices the atmosphere in the room changing; he senses that something palpable is descending toward him, physically palpable. Instantly his thinking is blocked and everything arrives at once: contact, images, biographical information, all of these precise details that he himself could never know.

In general, the way that the deceased left is fairly clear because it is the last thing they recall. They start with the end, then follow the thread of their existence back up. Like a film in reverse that the mediums must put back in order.

As I push him to try and describe to me again and again what is happening to him, Pierre goes back to his animal side. In a séance, to successfully make contact, he says he must become a child again. We all still have a child within us, he reminds me, a very instinctive child who captures everything, absorbing everything the other people are feeling. As an adult, he has principles, knowledge, expectations, a daily life. In general, he knows what motivates each of his actions and his slightest gestures. No surprises. Nothing unexpected. Everything is done very consciously for an adult. Mediumship invites a person to return to the unawareness of childhood. Expect nothing, predict nothing, suppose nothing, and absorb everything, the way an animal absorbs everything in his environment: information, threats, etc. We call this "survival instinct" in animals, but in reality it is putting this enormous energy in action that allows us to know everything about what surrounds us. This happens spontaneously, without us thinking.

When Pierre receives clients as a healer, his therapeutic side is very pronounced. He instantly feels his patient's weak point. He goes straight there because he sees the diseased organ or body part. The weak point, the flaw that he enters into right away, is an obstructed image, like an Xray. Then he takes care of trying to fix the health problem in question.

"Instinct," "sixth sense," "mediumship," all of these different words describe this same state of the brain when it lets go and becomes completely intuitive, entirely available to information. English biologist Rupert Sheldrake has published remarkable works on this subject, showing the dominant role that the consciousness plays in behaviors observed in nature.[13]

---

13 Rupert Sheldrake, *Morphic Resonance: The Nature of Formative Causation*, Park Street Press, 2009.

But how, in this context, does one let go while still being able to make the distinction between one's imagination and real perceptions? For Pierre, the imagination relies on things we have experienced, that we already know, whereas perceptions lead us into the unknown. He discovers them at the same time that he becomes aware of them. The difficulty, he concedes, is that to be understood, these perceptions pass through the filter of his own experiences, his life. This is where someone really has to be anchored to practice this profession. Having this responsibility of distributing information requires being stable and of a clean spirit, for each word could construct or deconstruct the person who is hearing them.

The human being is capable of perceiving all of the energies in which he lives without even realizing it: energies of the ground, the magnetic world, energies of the universe, etc. We are all receptors. As long as we are unaware of it, as long as we don't realize who we are and what our potential is, we remain in rough perception.

This is not really what Pierre has been showing me since we started. In his two little rooms, the séance continues. After all of the details mentioning family, the war, and the past, my father arrives at his own life.

"Why am I being told about a windmill?

"I don't know . . . maybe because that's where he lived."

"He lived in a windmill?"

"No, but it was called that." My parents lived in the country, in a place known as the Windmill.

"He's talking a lot about books . . . He was interested in a lot of different things? It's like he always had the desire to learn. A researcher, always a scholar. Knowing things so he wouldn't be surprised."

"That's accurate."

"Yes, this man has a lot of character. He wasn't necessarily very accessible, though."

"No."

"But still open to discussion. When he was closed off, though, he really was . . . He had a problem with the survival of the soul?"

"What do you mean?"

"It wasn't something he believed in. But he really liked asking questions, understanding themes . . . transmitting, he liked to transmit things."

"Yes."

"Because he's someone who transmitted what he knew, who educated other people, was that the case?"

"Yes."

"That's his profession, eh? That's what I'm hearing. I see him with a feather in his hand, a feather pen. He likes study-ing. He likes learning. He's a man who educates other people, an instructor, a teacher."

"Yes."

"It was his passion."

My father adored his teaching career, and a number of his former students still have fond memories of his history-geog-raphy classes. In addition to painting, writing also meant a great deal to him. It is from being close to him that I learned to write.

"A first name with an 'L' like Lucien, Louis, does that mean anything to you?"

"Yes. His father's name was Louis."

"His father, okay. His father was a bit rough, is that right? There's a kind of emptiness toward the father . . . did his fa-ther have a mustache?"

"Yes, I think so."

"He's behind him . . . There's something lacking in terms of the father. As if they weren't close, as if he wasn't there very often. He must have felt his absence in him. He missed his father, it's strange . . . He never said this?"

"Not really, no."

"There is perhaps a phase in his life that you don't know as much about, when he was between fifteen and twenty-five years old. A more muddled period . . . But he doesn't talk a lot, this man doesn't really feel like talking."

My grandfather Louis was a nice man, but larger than life to those who knew him. A manner that was a little cold, probably distant, and a posture that must have been no stranger to the continual suffering his war injury inflicted on him. My mother, who spoke about this with my father's mother, thinks that Louis must not have been present the way a father should be for his son. His only son. A troubling fact that echoes in what Pierre is capturing this very minute. My father had stopped confiding in his mother at the age of nine. He had stopped, walled inside his silence, and would no longer share anything about himself. At nine years old.

"He's someone you could discuss any subject with, but who would not offer up anything emotional. He had an emotional hypersensibility that he controlled all his life. Was he also impulsive?"

"Yes, that is true."

"Explosively impulsive, sometimes even a little violent?"

"Yes."

"Did he have anger in him?"

"I don't know."

"He's a nice guy, but there was an anger in him. As if he was always swallowing all of his resentment?"

"Yes . . ."

"Did he not have a problem with his finger?"

"I don't know."

Among the revelations that my mother will make to me when we dissect the transcription of this séance together is the episode during which, in a fit of anger, my father had punched a wall . . . and broken his finger. The fact that Pierre mentions my father's "explosive and sometimes violent impulsivity" and continues by mentioning a "problem with his finger" is striking all the same. For despite everything, these outbursts by my father were far from common. He was not a violent man. Temper tantrums, yes, but that kind of explosion of anger only happened one time.

With no further instructions from me, the past still seems to come flooding back in the person of that uncle, who was also mentioned by Henry Vignaud.

"Does he have an uncle, a cousin who disappeared?"

"Disappeared, what do you mean by that?"

"We think that he's no longer here, but we're not sure."

"Yes."

"A long time ago."

"Yes, but do you have any more details?"

"He's been on the other side for a very long time."

"Oh really?"

"It wasn't an accident, is that your understanding?"

"Um, well . . ."

"He was killed. I have something like a murder, an assassination, but he also had a gun . . . I see him in a uniform, I see mud everywhere."

"Yes."

"A big coat, because it's cold, does that mean anything to you?"

"Yes."

"And now, *poof*, I see an explosion."

"Really?"

"There's a lot of noise, does that seem right?"

"That rings a bell, yes."

"It's a war, the trenches, the war of 1914."

"Yes."

"I see someone. He's part of the family?"

"Yes."

"It's not his father, a brother, a . . ."

"It's his uncle."

"It's his uncle? Yes, I said 'uncle' earlier."

This is true, Pierre started by asking if "an uncle or a cousin who had disappeared" meant anything to me. Once again, I am flabbergasted by the emergence of these kinds of details that Pierre knows nothing about. Furthermore, this is the second time that my father's uncle has presented himself to a medium during these tests. He had disappeared in combat, and Pierre is seeing him with a gun, in the mud, wearing a coat . . . and for good reason, because he disappeared February 18, 1915.

How could the arrival of the same people with different mediums be explained? The simplest answer is probably because they are there with my father.

"He really loved that man. He didn't really know him, he didn't see him a lot, but he really liked him, he was his hero. You see what I mean?"

"Yes."

My father hadn't known him because Paul had died twelve years before his birth. But this uncle had acquired a certain status in the family history. And he was a painter, too, which must have accentuated the kinship my father felt with him. He was not at all made for war, if anyone ever could be. His death had been a horrifying heartbreak for his younger sister Lise, my father's mother.

"They are together. Survival exists, that's what he wanted to say . . . It's funny, it's as if he had found his childhood, people that had been lost from view. Was someone taken prisoner?"

"I'm not sure. Maybe."

"First World War? It seems to be something to do with war. Yes, it's 1914–1918 again, that's for sure. I see horses, things like that. I have the image; the color is not the same, a paler energy."

"Oh really?"

"This man must have been wounded because I see a blonde woman with a nurse's armband . . . Was that man wounded?"

"Um . . . there was a man I'm thinking of who was wounded, yes."

"That's when it was, then . . . '14–'18?"

"Yes."

"It's not a grandfather?"

"My grandfather?"

"Yes, it's your grandfather because he's telling me, 'This is the grandfather.'"

"Yes."

"Was something of your grandfather's removed?"

"The end of his foot."

"Ah yes, a toe. Was it the right foot?"

"I'm not sure."

"I'm seeing him dead, it's a bit strange. He made it out, though?"

"Um, yes."

"He made it out but I'm seeing him as if he had died, as if this had killed him on the inside."

This was the case in a certain way. That wound to the foot would disable him for the rest of his life. He was barely twenty years old when he endured the horrors of the war in an artillery regiment, and then came a shell that mutilated him for eternity. But had he been a prisoner? I don't know.

Until today, my father has only managed once to spontaneously pass along the information that there was something important in his casket. And that had been with Christelle, who still was unable to give official names to these objects. I am well aware that my father is having difficulty communicating, but why isn't he able to explain more easily that the things are hidden? This remains a deep source of questioning for me. Isn't he thinking about this? Is he out to lunch? Or, on the contrary, is he aware of it but prefers to give other details beforehand?

What transforms in us when we die? Pierre puts forth a few very enlightening hypotheses.

"Pierre, do you know what happens at the moment when we die? What do we become? Imagine that I had a heart attack right now; I fall down, what happens?"

"Well, first of all you wouldn't know what was happening. You're still in the moment of this interview."

"Really? Even though I may already be dead?" I exclaim with a laugh.

"I'll tell you later . . . no, don't worry. What I mean is that if at this very minute you had a heart attack, you would continue your interview without realizing it. You would realize you were dead when, after a time, you noticed a disconnect with your physical body. You would suddenly see yourself from above, and you would see me trying to give you CPR."

"Jeez . . ."

"If your death is sudden you don't notice it. But seeing your body after a certain time can help you become aware that it has happened."

"And what if, despite seeing my body, I don't understand? Is that possible? What happens then?"

"Yes, it's possible. That's why on the old battlefields there are plenty of dead people walking around wondering, 'What am I doing here?' They may have been there since 1914. They have all died but nobody told them, and they're frozen in this state of incomprehension and don't realize what has changed around them. The day that someone enters into contact with them and remarks that they no longer have bodies and that they don't have any reason to be here anymore, they are freed."

"So there must be a ton of people wandering the streets!"

"Yes, a ton. But fewer in the streets than in the fields. That's where the wars and massacres took place. Where people died violently without expecting it."

"And when we die at the hospital?"

"There we expect it, we know it's coming. And the sorrow of other people is also an indication. Another important element in becoming aware that we are dying is the constant presence of someone who comes to look for us so they can accompany us. I often draw a parallel with birth. When we come into the world, we are greeted: the midwife, our father if he's there, the family who holds us in their arms, etc. When we die, it's the same on the other side: as we're leaving our body, we are greeted by loved ones in exactly the same way."

"I would like to understand what I'm feeling psychologically once I realize what's happening to me. Let's use the same example: I have a heart attack, I die, I see myself from above, and I see you giving me CPR. Then what?"

"You're still you."

"OK, and I imagine I'll only have one thing on my mind: letting my wife and my daughter know."

"That's something the incarnated worry about."

"But my wife and my daughter, I . . ."

"You have to think 'disincarnated.' Even if you don't really feel like leaving your family, you will understand that it's a necessary law of your evolution, and of theirs. You will know then, obviously, that there is life after life. You will also know that you will be the one to come look for them when the time comes. You will finally discover that you will be able to intervene sometimes to help them. When all is said and done, what links you to them will not be changed. The only thing that will be different is that you will have answers that they will not yet have access to on their side."

"Yes, and I imagine that what could affect me most would be seeing them continually crying."

"Exactly. And at a given moment you will find a way of communicating with your daughter or your wife. This will be unique each time, as a function of their sensitivity and their way of being. You will come to them either in a dream, or in a more direct manner."

But does this mean that I can see them all the time? Are the people on the other side always watching us? Pierre says no. To see the living, the deceased have to come near them; they must destroy the veil that distances us from each other. On the other hand, a certain connection between us and them remains permanently. This way, when they feel that we are not doing well or that we need help, they are instantly nearby.

With this discussion I'm also hoping to understand what happens to the notion of the individual after death. Once we are dead, are we still ourselves?

Is my father still my father?

I am well aware that this question may seem absurd, and it's one I am becoming slightly obsessed with, but at the same time, even in our life on earth we can be very different people after intervals of just a few years. In what way, then, does death affect our individuality? Our identity?

Pierre responds that as far as the individual that we are, we are no longer that person once we are on the other side. But at the same time, we become that person again whenever we come near the earthly world again.

We are no longer that person, but that individual is here, it is part of *us*, of our history.

The more the spirit approaches the earthly worlds, the more it becomes an individual entity once more. When it distances itself, the individual fades and the spirit blends into an ensemble.

Words are starting to fail me here.

The spirit always preserves the memory of what it was, not only the life it has just left, but also the memory of its other lives, when it has had several. Pierre uses the image of a drop of water: each drop is unique, it holds onto the individual memory of the path it has taken, the experiences it has had, but once it is back in the ocean, it will dissolve and become ocean again.

This almost philosophical image goes a little bit against what we hope for and even what we imagine when we think about life after death. We see ourselves very much alive, very much *ourselves*, with our personality intact.

In fact, we like ourselves very much.

It would really be a shame to no longer exist. But this is a human vision, a vision of an incarnated being, and one that is probably missing two or three essential pieces of information.

Pierre insists, however, that our identity is not lost, it is blended into a collective ensemble but still endures. The best proof of this is that the more the deceased draw near, the more they reappropriate their earthly identity: their bad character, their nervous or very relaxed behavior, the way of being they had when they were alive, which the medium feels when a communication is established.

They become again who they were when they approach to communicate with us.

In the end, death does not radically change the person if the deceased remains close to the earthly time period. There they conserve their identity, their character, and their flaws. A feeling of incompleteness or the rejection of death are liable to hold the person there.

But based on what Pierre is saying, the majority of people are transcended once they have passed onto the other side. They understand. Only the resistant ones are left, hanging on and refusing to let go.

Pierre emphasizes that not only do the living influence the deceased with the way they grieve, but the deceased also influence their loved ones who are still on earth.

They may not let go of them.

If a deceased person decides that they have not finished what there is to do, if there are still things left unsaid, if they need to say something, they may not let go and instead may have an influence on the people or feelings linked to this un-accomplished desire. They may become clingy. In fact, some of the dead will do all that they can in order to not let go. Their loved ones may, as a result, have the feeling of being held in a yoke of suffering, tears, or . . . immense love. "I think about him every day, every day." Hanging on this way allows the deceased to continue existing a little bit on earth and to turn their back on reality as they watch their past on a continual loop. But is that really their place?

Without even mentioning life after death, the process of grieving does not consist of *forgetting* the deceased, or no lon-ger thinking about them, any more than it consists of main-taining a merged relationship with the deceased, identical to what it was when they were alive. The process of grieving consists of working out a new relationship. A relationship with the same love, the same strength, but also one that integrates the absence caused by the departure. We will return to this question of grieving in detail and in a practical way in the final part of this book with psychiatrist Christophe Fauré.

For the time being, talking to the deceased is essential to liberate them, just as Christelle Dubois recommends. One could say, "Okay, I have accepted your leaving. I am asking you to free yourself and to go into your light." It is even enough to think this, there's no need to shout. In general, the sound will be heard. In the same way that the relationships between living people are sometimes imperfect, and communication is not always easy, it may be exactly the same between the living and the deceased. Emotions and feelings may also be restraints.

According to Pierre, the evolution of the deceased takes place on the other side. In the same way, they may help the people who remain, moving forward. What they did not learn on earth they are capable of learning through someone who is still there. Allowing a person on earth to move forward makes them move forward, too. As we can see, relationships and ties are not broken by death. This knowledge and clear realization offer us the possibility to suffer less from a death than the way we usually do today, and to make the separation a chance to continue growing on both sides. Death gives us the chance to reinvent our relationships; it only appears to be putting an end to them.

But *where* do the dead live? This question, too, is dizzying. Pierre proposes a few clues. They evolve into a matter different from ours. A world of matter in which there is neither space nor time. Displacements take place instantaneously, faster than a thought develops. It's a universe somewhat in the image of our own, in which they can recreate various worlds. It is difficult to conceive of this reality with our earthly imaginations. Feeling it, on the other hand, is possible. This is what people who have lived through a near-death experience have done. And even in their own testimonies they have a hard time explaining the experience with words. They feel that they acquired an understanding without anything being verbalized. Perhaps it would be useful for us to favor the use of techniques and methods that allow us to silence our minds and open our other senses to begin to comprehend the subtle world? Meditation, respiratory techniques, shamanic voyages . . . there are many methods to explore if we are to begin truly activating our intuitive skills. In this way, we could have the experience rather than learning about it.

The difficulty my father is having transmitting as clearly as I would expect from him is related to the fact that to do this, he needs to actually come back toward me, approach our universe again. Now, my father no longer has a body or vocal cords. On the other side, he has discovered another form of language for which words, his body, and his mouth are not useful in the slightest.

Thought is what connects beings.

They no longer speak; they are in permanent osmosis.

I need to get everything out of my head that has to do with a physical body and a world of matter; if I want to be able to have an approximate idea of my father's location today, I need to erase from my spirit these notions of time and space that are so essential to my idea of reality. And an idea of what that implies in terms of communication.

I don't need to try and speak with him; instead I should be trying to be in communion with him. For the interesting thing, as Pierre reminds me, is that all human beings on earth can communicate with spirits. Each one of us is capable of rediscovering this state of osmosis with our disappeared loved ones.

The love that connects us to them is the thread.

Fear interferes with things. Fear fashions a wall of negative energy that reinforces the irrational belief that there is nothing after death and no contact is real. Recognizing that our loved ones are alive opens the doors, and feeling them through ourselves is possible. Then the interferences are eliminated.

Why not let go of all of our beliefs? Alone, within ourselves, with no one to judge us, why don't we let these pretenses fall and liberate ourselves from our education, which prevents us from making our own experiences for ourselves? Why not try to open ourselves up and let what happens happen? This is not necessarily going to work on the first try, but why not see where it leads?

When you close this book, try for a moment not to think. Obviously, as soon as you try not to think, you won't be able to stop thinking about not thinking. To help yourself, fix your attention on an image, a waterfall, for example, and observe the things that emerge. It is by opening our internal world that the door to other external worlds opens. This is what Pierre has taught me today.

But I digress. Back to Papa. As with the others, the moment has come for me to help Pierre—and my father—focus on what we're interested in.

I slip in an initial indication while remaining relatively evasive: "You don't want to just ask him if there's something that stood out to him the moment he died, or the moment he was buried?"

"When he was dressed . . . they put on pants that were too short for him, but he didn't care . . . Someone had something for him, an envelope, he's showing a word on it. He's talking about a white or beige envelope, more off-white."

Here's the first thing that arrives immediately. Amazing! The note I put with the four objects was slipped inside an off-white, beige envelope. I decide to reinforce the validation to Pierre.

"Just before the funeral, I did something, and I talked to him about it. He and I have a deal."

"He'll give you a sign, don't worry."

"No, that's not it. He's supposed to tell you things . . . Things were actually placed in his casket. Can you ask him what they were?"

Pierre seems to be able to manage stress very well, so I went for it and took the risk of revealing to him a little more clearly the nature of the test, hoping that this would not make him lose his composure.

"Today he doesn't give a shit about his casket. I'm sorry, I'm being a little crude, but . . ."

"Yes, I know, but he does give a shit about the book we're working on."

"No . . . did you put three things inside?"

"I can't tell you anything."

"He's talking to me about three things . . . there's an object, there's a kind of homage in what you've done, there's also a kind of test."

"Ah yes, that's the test!"

"In the casket? It's funny to have thought of that at the time."

"About doing a test? Is that what he's saying?"

"Yes."

"He didn't like it?"

"It makes him laugh. He had a sense of humor, it's making him chuckle . . . There's something with some writing, like a book someone put on top of him. There's something like an envelope . . . ah yes, definitely. It's funny because he's also saying to himself, 'He should also put in a recording device!' This is funny!"

"A recording device, is he the one saying this to you?"

"Yes. That would have been funny, right?"

It would have been funny, but why is he able to say "recording device" and not "paintbrush" or "compass"? At the same time, he has just mentioned the envelope with the note that I wrote. And the book. I am as stunned as I was the first time, and at the same time I am expecting so much from myself and from him that during the course of the séance, I always notice first what he's not saying, and realize later what he has just given me. What do you expect, I'm a journalist.

"There's an object . . . something shiny. He's telling me that could have belonged to him."

"Yes."

"An object with a round shiny top. And there's something silky . . . like satin, does that make sense to you?"

"Yes."

"Beige or cream, I get the sense that it's padded."

"Yes. That's correct. But all caskets are."

"Not with cream or beige satin . . . There are hearts in his story, too. Someone who made hearts, writing? This story seems to be about love . . . Is there someone who put in an envelope?"

"I'm not going to answer you."

The off-white envelope Pierre saw in the beginning contains these few words: "I love you, Papa," and I signed it: "Your big boy." That's what my parents usually called me. Yes, what's in the envelope is "about love." And the fabric in his casket is a cream color.

"A sealed envelope," Pierre specifies.

"That's what you're seeing?"

"That's what he's telling me. It's inside . . . that's all I see."

"What are you feeling now, exactly? Are you seeing images?"

"It's more him talking to me, and he's sending me images, too."

"What's making you say that it's not thought transmission or telepathy that is allowing you to obtain all this information?"

"Because of the energy, the ambiance. And my internal feeling is totally different."

"Meaning?"

"Meaning that when I have intuitions, when I get information via clairvoyance, for example, it's totally different. In that case it's more like a self-evident fact that crosses my spirit. I don't think about it. With the deceased, I'm not thinking either, but they do it for me."

"How can you be sure that it's different?"

"The reception isn't the same. In clairvoyance, it's sudden, instantaneous. While with the deceased it takes more time. When I speak for them, it's not at all my character that expresses itself but that of the person in contact with me. That's where I see a real difference, because I really separate my character from the character of the deceased person I'm communicating with. And the more they come down, as I explained to you, the more they take on the personality they had when they were alive on earth."

"And why, if you're with him, doesn't my father clearly say, 'My son put this and this'?"

"Because he doesn't have all the words."

"Why not?"

"Because that demands energy, saying all the words, to form real sentences. For them and for me. I need energy to receive, and I don't have enough to pick up on everything. I see the images he's showing me, but it's not his words that I say, they're my words. He's not telling me, 'It's that.' He's showing me an image in the blink of an eye, it goes fast. Then, to understand, I really have to look for my own words. I have to capture the image while eliminating everything in me that interferes with it. To do that, I have to be able to no longer be me, and be him instead. It's this feeling that allows me to know that it has nothing to do with thought transmission or clairvoyance with you."

"So the dead don't speak?"

"Not all of them."

"Which means that there are some who manage to speak to you with words?"

"Yes, but those are very old."

"And why can't my father speak to you since you say that he's alive?"

"Because they have to create an energy vibration to create a sound inside me. He has to cross through all of the interference there is between the earth and the vibration where he is in order to create something fluid and audible. You can't imagine!"

"Uh, no, I can't imagine, no."

"And since his death is fairly recent, he doesn't possess all of these subtleties yet. Especially considering that he didn't believe any of this was real, that's the funny part."

"Is it possible that he didn't understand where he was?"

"That may happen but that's not the case with him."

"Oh no?"

"No, I would say more that he's someone who maybe hadn't finished what he'd started, or maybe hadn't told people in his family what he wanted to say. I have the sense of that energy more than anything else because at the moment he's set back, he's observing, and then suddenly he sends something along and then I see him smile."

"He must also learn how to communicate with you, then?"

"Yes . . . Is there a watch in the casket?"

"I can't answer you, you'll know later."

"I think there's a watch, it could be a fob pocket watch, an object he really loved."

"What's he saying to you?"

"He's talking about time, he loved time."

"Those are the words you have?"

"Yes. He's talking to me about time."

"You have to interpret what he sends you?"

"Exactly, the only people who may be mistaken are us, the mediums."

"Do you sense that he is impatient?"

"I felt smiles. A reserved smile."

"What about the test, what I did with the casket?"

"He found it shocking at first, then funny, very funny. He said you wouldn't change, professional until the end."

"But this was the chance . . ."

"It's funny, it's like I had a family photo with him in it. I saw it clearly. There's also the book, the writing, something coiled."

"And the object with the round top?"

"Yes, it's round, it could be a medal . . . or a compass?"

This séance has surprised me again, as Pierre so quickly sees the letter I left in the casket, the book, and the round object . . . Although over an hour before, walking down the street, I asked my father if he could choose to talk about the book by Dino Buzzati and the compass. But at the same time, Pierre's explanations and those of the other mediums are allowing me to understand better the complexity of what I am requesting from my father. In spite of everything, he's not doing that badly, is he?

Loan

Loan Miège is a young woman in her late thirties. She lives in Vaucluse, and she is not only a medium but also is in contact with an invisible world that is abundant and extraordinarily rich. In fact, Loan talks as much with the spirits of trees and nature in general as she does with deceased souls. In addition, she is a caregiver, accompanies other people, and teaches. Though at first I was incredulous about her many professions, I followed her into the forest and that changed everything. I realized then just how sincere Loan is, and that she is a person of rare integrity. A beautiful person, capable of things that are absolutely astonishing. Open to discussions and generous in her explanations, Loan allowed me to verify myself that what she told me about the invisible world of nature was perceivable. This was very impressive. Even though communication with the deceased does not make up the core of her profession, I asked her to participate in this test. Along with the séance, this would give me the chance to better discover her universe. I was not disappointed.

Loan had a unique childhood, but not for the reasons we might imagine in this book. There were no entities appearing in her childhood bedroom, no light guides, no perceptions. Just hell.

The hell of madness in which, to survive, she must completely muzzle her sensitivity.

Her father is schizophrenic, an alcoholic, and violent.

Her parents separated a few months after her birth. Of her social worker mother, Loan says she took her role a little too much to heart, to the point of moving into the difficult inner city of La Villeneuve in Grenoble, where poverty, violence, and drugs were rampant. Despite their separation, her parents saw each other and would have brief continuations of their relationship. Three years after Loan was born, a little brother arrived. An unwanted little boy. An abortion had been planned but Loan's mom refused at the last minute. The child soon shows signs of suffering from severe schizophrenia and today lives under the care of the state as a disabled person.

Their mom tried to maintain the fiction of an intact family, and let the children stay with their father every other weekend. Loan explains, "She thought it was good for us to see our father, probably because of her social work thing. In reality she was handing us over to the executioner."

Those years will damage Loan and her brother a great deal. The toxic insanity of this man will put them through an ordeal. The weekends with him become moments when all of Loan's energy becomes concentrated on a single goal: to survive.

The dad lives in the mountains, cut off from everything. He lives with a new girlfriend, the mother of a little girl who is five years old. Loan is six at the time, and her brother is three. During each of her father's fits, she takes the little girl and, holding her brother with her other hand, she flees into the forest, running as fast as she can. They stay there in hiding. At a very young age, Loan knew that her father was an extremely dangerous person.

Instinctively, she notices the signs leading up to one of his frenzies. The man is diagnosed as schizophrenic, but early on, Loan sees something in the way his fits occur that is more akin to possession. She feels that another being takes over her father's body. His gaze changes; he's no longer the same person. "He becomes a living demon," she recalls. Then he starts breaking everything, destroying everything around him.

To protect herself, Loan learns to be constantly on alert whenever she is in his presence, to be vigilant and detect the moment when the personality change happens so that she has enough time to leave. She is resigned to the fact that only running away can protect them from these moments.

His temporary fits are not the only problem. The man also has personality-change problems that are more long-term. There is one memory that remains very present and painful, going back to when Loan was fourteen.

While the children are at his house, the dad gets the idea for a tourist trip to the châteaux of Bavière. A ten-day excursion.

Ten days of total hell.

The trip has barely started, and already the father is behaving like a Nazi officer plunged right back into the Third Reich. For ten days, he and the children live in Nazi Germany. He rations the food because "it's wartime" and spouts anti-Semitic remarks and death threats. Loan, whose mother is of Jewish descent, is nervous that her father will remember because he keeps repeating how "they must be killed."

Today, Loan explains that during this trip, her father was, in her opinion, literally invaded by the wandering soul of a Nazi officer. He was no longer himself. He was ready to put an end to his days, the same way the officers and dignitaries of the regime had done, the only difference being that he intended to lead his children into death along with him.

One day, he enters the highway on the wrong side. Loan remembers the experience with terror. She feels like she's going to die. But while the car is continuing its crazy path, something happens that even today Loan still cannot understand. Suddenly, time slows down. She thinks that death is coming for her, that it's all over. Though she never received any religious education, she begins to pray. A prisoner in the car, she calls for help, saying that she and the two other children have done nothing wrong and didn't ask for this to happen to them. They want to live. It's not fair. She prays with her entire soul, with all of her strength, and "at some point there were clouds underneath the car, I felt it lifting up, then it fell back down onto the road and my father became human again, if we could call him that." The family reaches a hostel where everyone falls asleep. What happened? Here we find ourselves within the confines of the unexplained.

Loan grew up in the midst of insanity, obliged to barricade herself so as to not be caught up in it. But as soon as she becomes an adult and is finally able to leave this family situation, she begins to perceive the deceased. This happens for the first time when she is nineteen with a visit from her great-grandmother, with whom Loan had kept very close ties, who had died three years before. Loan was always a very sensitive child, but this particularity was only expressed through the painting and sculpting she has practiced assiduously since her childhood. She cannot allow herself to go further. Too much danger. As an independent adult she finally allows herself to open up.

Loan's life is disconcerting. She has had the experience of suffering, fear, and the most terrifying madness, all while preserving the formidable spiritual force that had always been curled up inside her and then allowing it to bloom. In this small delicate body, behind those joyful and mischievous eyes, is an old power.

We meet in Paris. I place the photo on the table. Loan looks at it. The contact seems to occur immediately.

"He is deceased, I'm guessing?"

"Yes."

"A heart issue? Right away I'm feeling pressure on the heart. And I'm feeling a lot of sadness in him. He's someone who must have lost someone very close to him . . . It's as if there was a sort of grief that he was never able to get over . . . Now on the other hand, on the other side, he's accompanying you. He managed to integrate the lessons he learned during his earthly life to transcend himself and be at peace. He is more in sync with his spirit, his own inner light. I feel like he is at peace and smiling . . . all of a sudden I really feel a distance between the man in this photo and the one I'm capturing. In the photo, he has this pain, this suffering. He is sad, and doesn't speak. I sense someone closed in on himself, someone modest who lives with suffering so as not to disturb other people. This weighs on him inside; it's something hard to express. I'm being shown that this man coughs a lot. Did he have problems with his lungs? I feel a sort of pressure throughout my whole chest. I'm being shown mucus, things that aren't able to be expelled . . . I'm telling you everything that's coming to me, all right?"

"Of course, yes."

Having read about my father's medical details in previous chapters, you will no doubt appreciate the accuracy of these remarks. Loan is capturing a whole range of physical and emotional parameters that correspond completely with my father's history. His health, his heart, his lungs . . . and this inextinguishable grief. Grief for my brother.

"He's strong . . . well, I don't really know what I'm saying, if it's true or false, but it's what's coming to me."

"That's very accurate. And even if something seems absurd to you, don't hesitate to say it."

"All right . . . because now, I'm seeing three children. Why am I being shown these children? I have the sense that there was an accident, that it was very painful for this man and he never really got over it."

Loan doesn't know that it's my father at this point. And indeed there were three of us, Thomas having died in Afghanistan in 2001.

"This man . . . it's as if he has the feeling that he had a curse on him and at the same time there's something bright, hope . . . How can I put this? I sense that he's a very handy guy, he likes to do things with his hands and what he creates with his hands helps him hang onto life. It gives him a kind of hope. As if this relieved him of this burden, this weight, and these constraints he had a hard time handling. He would have liked things to be different, and with this manual work, he escapes. He has the sense of transcending what is painful and making something beautiful and useful out of it. Something beyond all earthly heaviness . . ."

Here again, what exactness. My father maintained a cathartic relationship with painting. Since he was incapable of expressing his emotions verbally, the act of painting had become a way for him to remove himself from the problems of existence. Alone in his studio all day long, he would paint, his nose stuck to his paintbrush, and put the world in parentheses. Each emotion that would not come out of him would be literally transformed into matter in his paintings: the lines, the brushstrokes, the colors.

Without my interrupting her, Loan continues with the same momentum.

"I hear a first name, but first names aren't my thing, so I don't really know what to think about it. I have the first name Jean coming. I don't know who Jean is, if it's him or someone else."

"Very good."

Once again, Loan doesn't know that it's my father in the photo, nor that his first name is Jean-Pierre. She is impressive.

"Now, I have more things about him on the other side. He says he's taking part in this book because he suffered a great deal because of this doubt, because of this internal agony he felt during his earthly life and that, in passing to the other side, he has really come to understand that there was something else, that it was luminous and that life had a purpose. This purpose that he had such a hard time perceiving had been such a burden on his shoulders during his earthly life. Once he passed to the other side, he realized that things had a purpose. That one has to hold on, it's important. This is what he wants to show. Hold on and enjoy life, that's what's most important. He has regrets about this. Because of the weight he was carrying, he must not have enjoyed life the way he could have. He closed himself off on his own a little bit. Today, now that he's passed to the other side, he's aware of this and he is happy to be able to share his experience, his transformation. He's talking about 'transformation' . . . It's a bit like he wanted to testify and at the same time be a kind of example to show that even though we may be locked in on earth, we are far more than we imagine."

I listen in silence. I'm not able to judge the truth of what Loan is describing to me about my father on the other side, but considering the accuracy of what she reports about him before his death—"He suffered greatly from this doubt, this internal agony . . . He had a hard time perceiving the purpose of life, that it was a burden on his shoulders . . . He was a little bit closed off on his own . . ."—I can assess what my father has realized since his departure. And I decide to share this with Loan.

"I'm very happy that he's taking part in this the way he is."

"I feel joy, enthusiasm on his part. I'm asking him if he wants to say something else."

But while the séance seems to be unfolding perfectly, I am about to make a blunder. Having already done the same thing with Christelle did not teach me a lesson.

"I asked him something before I came, did he hear me?"

"That's making him laugh . . . He's telling me he did hear."

Nearly two decades of contact with her father's madness marked Loan permanently. More surprisingly, the proximity of all of this danger gave her the sense that schizophrenia is a poorly-experienced mediumship.

Loan is convinced that her brother and her father are mediums but that they are not able to manage it. She says her father also went through extreme suffering, that he was beaten and had had a terrible childhood. This created enormous weakness in him, and through these gaping wounds the malicious entities would penetrate and take possession of him. Many people who qualify as "schizophrenics" could be, in the same way, mediums overwhelmed by their perceptions.

Why, in such an environment, did Loan not slip into schizophrenia herself? Did her strong character play a role? Did the responsibility she felt to protect her brother help her stay anchored?

A few years ago my friend Paul Bernstein and I published the *Extraordinary Experiences Clinical Handbook*. This foundational text for INREES[14] is a collective effort, regrouping and presenting in categories a large number of extraordinary experiences listed to date, as well as suggestions for therapeutic approaches. It is intended for health professionals,

---

14 See www.inrees.com.

psychologists, and psychotherapists of various kinds, but also for the general public, people who have had one or several of these experiences, or the people around them who are trying to understand the changes in behavior that are affecting their loved one; in fact, it is intended for anyone who has seen or heard about these experiences and who desires to know and understand what serious scientific research and clinical studies of these experiences have allowed us to discover.

We especially considered the reality of the existence of a clear distinction between *madness* and *normality*. Unanimously, all of the contributors to the *Handbook* had admitted that such a border does not exist. We had also summarized their thoughts by writing: "There exists a kind of continuum between disease and health. In peaceful conditions, in people who are not suffering from any particular injury, the human psyche will function in a balanced manner, or, let's say, an appropriate manner. Whenever a slight trauma occurs, there will be a slight destabilization, then a return to equilibrium; with a more intense trauma, deeper layers or structures will be shaken, which will also disturb the equilibrium, until the point when a catastrophic trauma will shatter the personality into pieces (a depressive breakdown, delirium, for example). A person who has never shown signs of psychological problems is not necessarily a balanced person. . . . Only life will show the truth. One must, therefore, rely on time and the proof that comes later. Besides, even at the heart of pathological personalities, there remain 'islets of health.' It is in fact thanks to them that the individual can recover his health with the help of therapists who will help him reinforce them, develop them, and rely on them."[15]

---

15 See chapter 2 of Stéphane Allix and Paul Bernstein (eds.), *Expériences extraordinaires. Le manuel clinique*, Dunod/InterEditions, 2013.

In summary, the perceptions of mediums may be a good experience, or they may inversely provoke a complete breakdown, frenzies, and significant psychological problems in a person made fragile by particular psychic injuries. Between these two extremes we encounter a whole range of attitudes and reactions. None of the mediums I met have escaped these moments of uncertainty, doubt, danger, and learning.

The example of Loan confirms this observation. With time, she used the presence of her father and brother's schizophrenia in her life as what she calls a "training ground."

At times, she herself was afraid of succumbing to it. She felt that this was possible. She was lucky to have had the strength to return to her life. In those moments of danger, she was indeed able to realize that she had to face her sufferings and undergo a process of internal healing. She realized that flaws and emotional fragility exist in every person, and if they are not addressed, the risk remains that other entities will slip in and now and then take possession of us. This is not necessarily noticeable or even visible. This penetration, except in extreme cases like her father's, is sly, discreet, and unconscious, but also effective, as we have seen.

To avoid giving in to these external forces while maintaining the possibility of a controlled opening, Loan started working on identifying, understanding, and healing her wounds. She worked on accepting her life on earth, instead of floating up there. The people who are sucked into madness are those who feel overwhelmed and who do not have the strength, the assistance, or the resources to exercise this beneficial lucidity, which is a prerequisite for any path to healing.

The insane are persuaded that they are not insane.

Among the patients she sees—she cares for and meets with people regarding both physical and spiritual issues—many of them display these kinds of problems. Mediumship that is difficult to manage, or family problems linked to these kinds of things. Today she is no longer afraid of mental illness. She knows its contours and the way it expresses itself. Also, whenever a patient comes to see her saying they have been possessed, or that they are hearing voices, she is on familiar ground and feels equipped to go looking for the reasons behind these things. Behind the image she presents as a gentle and delicate young woman, Loan is also a warrior. How else could she have gone through what she went through to get here today? Loan turned her childhood into a source of strength. Her relationship with her family is still complicated—she no longer sees her father, in fact. "He's someone who is much too dangerous to be around, absolutely unmanageable. He doesn't recognize at all that he has a problem, he thinks he's omnipotent." On the other hand, her little brother is extremely gentle and kind, when he is on his medication.

Confronted by this reality of suffering, Loan is also very pragmatic. She is the first one to recognize that the first step toward the process of inner healing is beyond the good intentions of schizophrenics.

It is beyond the intentions of her brother. Today, only medication prevents him from suffering. It does not fix the problem—it is not made for that—but is there to minimize suffering, which is already invaluable for someone who is ill. Also, we must not forget that this is simply a lid that is being put over real problems that demand to be treated. Closing our eyes to this does not constitute a long-term solution.

I asked many psychiatrists about the distinction they make between insanity and extraordinary perception. The majority of them truly touched me with the honesty of their answers. Not one confirmed to me that what the insane see does not exist. But they all immediately added that for a psychiatrist, the question of the reality or illusion of the experiences their patients reported was very secondary, in the end.

The first question they ask themselves is, "Is my patient suffering or not? Are the voices he says he's hearing in his head bothering him or not?" In the case of suffering, they work to reduce this; as a nearly general rule this is done with medication, because there is no other option to respond to the urgency of the situation. They are aware that their prescription does not heal, but it quiets the voices, the delirium, everything that is unbearable for the sick person. This is the problem for Loan's brother: he is potentially dangerous, and only strong doses of medication that knock him out prevent him from becoming a threat to himself or other people.

Wouldn't the solution be to look for the deep-rooted causes of the disease? This is the opinion of a growing number of health professionals who, going beyond the immediate therapeutic response to suffering, are attempting, via approaches that are sometimes quite varied, to identify the causes of these sometimes immeasurable fragilities that affect their patients. Even if this means that their inquiry leads them toward the invisible world. These physicians, psychotherapists, and psychologists are admirable pioneers. It was to bring together the knowledge we had acquired across the world and to make them better known in France that Paul Bernstein and I had started writing the *Clinical Handbook*. It was for this same reason that I founded INREES.

These people I mention are pioneers, and unfortunately, the care for the mentally ill in everyday life is something that at times is considered absurd in France. Loan is disappointed to have never to this day met a psychiatrist with whom she could have a discussion about what she senses, her intuitions. She has observed with her brother that too often, the urgency of the response to his suffering takes precedence over any attempt at reflection.

We silence the symptoms, and that's enough.

As a result of her insistence to try and find a solution to heal her brother, the psychiatrist caring for the young man came up with no better response for Loan than a kind of threat: "You yourself could develop schizophrenia after thirty years and your children will run the risk of having it, too." At the time, this announcement provoked a cataclysm inside Loan. Suddenly her life was damned. How sad it was to be called a "caregiver" and to be so devoid of kindness and emotional intelligence! There is nothing more disconcerting than being exposed to ignorance camouflaging itself behind certainties. It took time for Loan to regain her confidence after this detestable interaction and to understand why she herself would not tumble into madness.

It is true that with the unthinkable childhood she had had, I once asked myself how she could welcome the emergence of her own perceptions. Having witnessed her father's illness, hadn't she been afraid at age nineteen, when she saw her great-grandmother appear before her, that she was becoming schizophrenic herself? Her response was completely in line with what we published in the *Clinical Handbook*: one must not impose a diagnosis based on the *content* of an extraordinary story, but on the *manner* in which it is expressed.

In fact, when her deceased great-grandmother appeared to her for the first time, the gentleness of the experience left Loan with the strong sensation that she was not having a fit like her father, but simply living something else. The calm of what she experienced then was a clear sign that she was not in the process of going insane. She recognized the vibration of her great-grandmother and felt that the old lady was there to help her.

Loan is moved by something even greater. She is carried by a light and senses the luminous beings that are around her. With a laugh, she concedes that precisely by saying that she makes herself sound a little schizophrenic, but the difference lies in the fact that she knows how to utilize her perceptions to help others, to build, to make things better. To do good.

From all of this we can glean that it does not make any sense to categorically reduce schizophrenia to hallucinations and mediumship to real perceptions. Schizophrenics and mediums have access to the same invisible world. The former go there and lose their way, and the latter go there and come back as they please.

This observation does not change much for the current care of those with mental illnesses. Loan's inability to help her brother is a daily lesson in humility. "I did not manage to save him," she says when she talks about him.

Feeling confident because of how easily she connected with my father, and since it seems that both of them are encouraging me, I begin to explain to Loan the objective of this séance.

"I asked him to tell you something."

"Ah, okay . . . that puts a little pressure on me. And as soon as there's a bit of stress, all of the perceptions go into a panic."

"But there's no reason for you to panic."

"So he has to tell me something?"

"Yes."

"Yep, there it goes. It's the stress . . . It's terrible but I'm blocked."

Thinking I was helping Loan hone in on a more specific goal, all I have really done is disturb her. And she begins to lose the fluidity of the connection she and my father had established.

"I put several things in his casket and I'm asking him to tell the mediums what they were."

"All right."

"I'm well aware that it's not easy. But he will be able to do it once you are a little less tense . . . Also, don't hesitate to tell me even the most unexpected things that come to you. For the time being, I suggest we go onto another subject: can you ask him to describe the people he found after his death?"

"I see that he really succeeded in passing through each stage to get to the luminous area where he is more in connection with beings who will teach him and allow him to continue advancing."

"But he's . . . does it bother you if I ask you questions?"

"No, on the contrary, go ahead."

"Is what you're seeing coming directly from a living being or do you have the sense that you're accessing this information through him?"

"I see a silhouette. As if he has passed through different steps of evolution; he lost his incarnated form, his identity. He's beyond the person he was, he has passed all of that. Now it's more a silhouette, a mass of energy, and I sense his presence."

"Can you hear him saying words? Are you seeing images? How is what you're receiving manifesting itself?"

"I get everything at the same time. I also have to pay very close attention because it's passing through my filters and it could be distorted. It's the interpretation that's always the problem."

"Distorted in what way?"

"The information passes through me, through my experience, my internal bank. Speaking with a deceased person is a little like word of mouth; after a while the initial information might be slightly altered."

"He's saying words to you?"

"Every so often, yes."

"So why is it that if he's here, living, you can't hear sentences, ask questions, and get a long answer, for example?"

"I think it's more related to my stress, because when he talks to me I hear him. But the challenge in what we're doing now is increasing my stress, and that acts as a filter and makes things much more muddled."

"But why does stress do that? If I'm talking in front of you now, whether you're stressed or not you will hear me perfectly. What is different with him?"

"It doesn't pass through the same channels. We can say that I *hear* things he's saying to me, but it's not physical, it's not my eardrum vibrating and transmitting the information to the brain. In this case, it's a much more subtle wave that is captured by a different sense called 'clairaudience.' And if my energetic bodies are interfered with because I'm feeling stressed, the information I pick up this way will either be modified, altered, or even blocked. It's a little like a radio set that you put behind an electromagnetic field. The set can no longer receive anything."

"But then, how can you be sure that what you picked up in the beginning, for example, wasn't already distorted?"

"I can't be certain. The only way to be sure comes from validation, validation from you, for instance, of the information I gave. The doubt is always there. And in a way that's a good thing, because once we start to have certainties, we may make even more mistakes."

"But haven't you developed inner tools to validate what you're feeling for yourself? Because when you started the séance, you described a lot of things without once asking me if it was accurate or not. You seemed really confident."

"Yes, that's true. It's actually because it came to me like an avalanche, like a waterfall. And when it comes like that, without any will on my part, it's a good sign. It means that it's not coming from my imagination, or from something I'm projecting, but instead it is truly coming from the person asking to express themselves."

"How can you feel the difference?"

"It imposes itself on me. I feel like I'm being pushed."

"So you have to find a way to calm yourself as much as you can so you can be available to what's coming."

"Yes."

"I'm going to suggest an exercise for you: try to relax, to create the void, and I'm going to ask you something about the man in the photo. Do you think, spontaneously, you will be in a better position to capture what he says?"

"We can try, yes."

As she talks about her worlds and the beings she perceives, Loan is always very careful not to identify herself with them. The feelings, emotions, and ideas she captures are not her own. Attentive to her anchoring, she knows that forgetting even for an instant to maintain a watertight barrier between herself and the invisible forces who are present would expose her—as it would us in a similar situation—to the risk of leaving her body completely and becoming a puppet animated by external forces.

A schizophrenic.

She agrees with Pierre Yonas when he mentions the sometimes harmful influence that may exist between the living and the deceased. Loan suspects that many people labeled as "depressives" are influenced, without realizing it, by deceased people who are suffering. These people are not aware this is happening, often because they don't believe in it themselves. Medication allows them to curb their sensations, and then they have the impression that they are doing better, but the problem is not solved. The emotional and energetic dependency is still there.

This misreading of the influence of energetic links between the worlds of the living and the spirits comes from the fact that in the West, the invisible world is not recognized as being something real. However, in a number of cultures, one's relationship with one's ancestors is part of life. These phantoms are lived with every day.

In the West, being cut off from this spiritual reality, the majority of people who die do so imagining that there's nothing afterwards. They disembark in the beyond without knowing what to do, without having been prepared for it, and having received no help from the living people they were close to. This is because their loved ones did not imagine it would be useful to speak to the deceased, either, since they're dead.

By closing ourselves off from the existence of the invisible world, we are suffering, for it is real. It runs throughout our own reality and affects each one of us.

Loan is more or less always in a state of perception. This ability is never completely switched off in her. As a result, sometimes she is spontaneously seized by deceased people asking her for help. In a séance things are different, more prepared and expected. The arrival of the deceased evokes in her the sensation of a landing. As if there had been nothing and one second later something comes down and thickens. It's a little like all of the particles in the air became a sort of vapor, denser than we had originally believed. This thickening is accompanied by the sensation of a presence, a weight next to her.

In Loan's séances, the expression of a deceased person usually coincides with the mention of the deceased by the client she is working with, as if entering into resonance with the deceased person provoked its manifestation. This is not fortuitous. In Loan's work, the deceased comes because it's going to have a direct link with the therapeutic process that is under way.

The unique thing about Loan is that she creates contact with other kinds of spirits. The spirits of the deceased are not the only ones whose moods rub off on us. There are others. Many others.

The visible and the invisible function as mirrors of each other.

In the visible world, millions of animal, vegetable, and even mineral species cohabitate. Going back to the most ancient knowledge of her ancestors, Loan explains that the same diversity exists in the invisible world. The two worlds, these two facets of reality, are each as rich and abundant as the other.

And there is no border between these two worlds.

There is no border between the visible and the invisible.

These two realities are open to one another. This is more and more the case because the earth's energy is changing, Loan believes. Duality is an illusion. Theoretically, the visible world is not separated from the invisible world. Also, in a sort of grand movement to find this original unity, the two worlds, distanced from each other in our current reality, are now, at this very moment, in the process of coming closer to each other. In fact, Loan explains, the visible world represents that of manifestation, and the matter in which we are able to experience this separation between objects and beings. This allows us to live in various situations, to develop and find access to a certain kind of knowledge. The invisible world is everywhere, omnipresent. We only perceive the visible, but our invisible part is far more expansive. Since we have lost contact with this invisible part of reality, we have identified ourselves too closely with matter. It is high time that we find our essence and our grandeur again.

Matter is only a learning space. We are above all celestial beings who have come to have an earthly experience. This is true for everything that is living: a human body, a vegetable, a stone, etc.

So, the person we have been communicating with since the beginning of this test, this person who sometimes struggles to make himself understood, is it no longer *my father* but *his essence*? The celestial being who had been hiding behind Jean-Pierre Allix all those years?

Loan, who studied biology, proposes a parallel with thermodynamics. In this discipline we talk about three states: the gas state, the liquid state, and the solid state.

Her parallel is based on the idea that the soul, or the being in its essence, finds itself in the gas state. It's a gas, so evanescent, and we don't see it. Yet it is there. But it is invisible.

When the being descends into the belly of a mother, the gas passes very easily to the liquid state. In the mother's belly, the environment is liquid, down to the structure of the being: even the bones resemble jelly more than anything else. This liquid state will progressively solidify into the fetus, then continue after birth and up until the age of twenty-one. In fact, it's not until age twenty-one that we achieve solidification of the tiniest bones in our hands and feet.

And then we arrive at adult age and finally at the solid state. A state that we conserve for several decades depending on our health. Then around the age of sixty or seventy, depending on the person, with the onset of aging we return again to a liquid state. We have circulation problems, we retain water, and progressively the body liquefies to go back to the gas state, physical death.

From this point of view, we realize that we are part of a natural cycle; there is no longer a visible or an invisible, only a cycle with different states that allow us to evolve.

I understand better why my father, now that he is in the gas state, sometimes has difficulty sharing information with mediums, beings that are in the solid state.

Most surprising is that he manages to do it at all.

This is probably due to the fact that he has preserved the memory of many essential points in his life. His memories are a part of his apprenticeship. We will return to the notion of the individual that I explored already with Pierre.

At the beginning of the test, I imagined that I would contact my father and he would be the same as he had been when he was alive. When I think about him, I see his face, I remember his emotions, his words. In other words, I am still fixated on the personality I was familiar with, on the path of his earthly life, having, in the end, a very limited image of him. I keep hearing from all of these mediums the same idea that the *person* answering us is quite real and quite alive—I no longer have a shadow of a doubt on that subject—but my memory of my father is probably rather different from what he has become again, now that he is unconstrained by the earthly plane. The individual participating in the test is still my father, I can feel it—I sense this link, his love for us—but at the same time he seems to be much more than the man I lived beside all those years. I imagine him immense and unknown.

And what do I know about the immense being living inside of *me*? Now that's a good question. It could be the subject of an entire book, but I can already tell that only undertaking a spiritual journey allows us to access this dimension of light and to learn a little more about the celestial being buried within us.

Why do we have so little access on earth to this being that is so vast, and why do we only become aware of our essence once we are dead? Loan continues her rather destabilizing explanation, but it is also one that hits the nail right on the head. If we do not have conscious and immediate access to this being, it is because it is buried under superfluity. And this superfluity is, paradoxically, what we believe to be our profound identity.

This is what is called "me."

In general, we adore "me." We always want to make it happy and never want to leave it. It's so cool to be "me" that that's what we'd like to be for eternity.

Well, that individual appears to be completely artificial.

It is only made up of *reactions*.

The cultural, social, familial, historical, transgenerational, and other contexts in which we are born and grow up are what creates this "me," a person endowed with a nature, fears, desires, phobias, a distinct viewpoint on far too many things, feelings, and emotions. Is "me" really that fragile? When all is said and done, does "me" exist only because it has been fashioned exclusively as a reaction to its environment?

"Me" is not at all going to like us thinking that about it.

"Me" does not agree.

Yet days, months, and years go by, and our essence has less and less of a chance to express itself because the individual who is fashioning themselves takes up far too much space. Fairly early on, generally over the course of childhood, our essence becomes inaccessible. "Me" appears proudly and starts to hold forth, usually starting in the play area at nursery school.

Why wait until death to liberate ourselves from this artificial construction and offer ourselves the chance to reconnect with our essence? Why wait until death to reunite with ourselves? Wouldn't being able to reconnect while we're still alive on earth help us to live our lives more fully? To understand the difficult things that happen to us? To develop rather than suffer? And have we not discovered since the beginning of this book that the work on ourselves that we perform during our life is prolonged after death, allowing us to exercise more discernment there and to enter into that place more calmly?

Let's go a little further into detail about what happens at the moment of death. Why do we have everything to gain by being prepared for it? After death—after the physical body has ceased to function—the subtle energies gather together to form a coherent ensemble that is able to gradually detach from its flesh vehicle. This stage takes a certain length of time, sometimes several days, and even longer if the person is not prepared at their departure into the beyond.

The soul, then, is waiting for the process to arrive at completion. It follows its body and attends its funeral. Once these things are done, it finds itself on what is called an "earthly" plane, one that is materially invisible but present all the same in the reality of living people. Loan explains that at that moment, different paths are available to the soul after this state. To demonstrate what she means, she proposes a few examples of possible routes.

Let's take the case of a soul in suffering before death who is not able to see beyond this suffering. It will replay this painful scene in a loop, like a broken record, and remain trapped by its own projections until it becomes aware of them. This soul is in definite need of assistance, whether it be from prayers by their loved ones or the intervention of luminous beings who can provide this kind of help. As another example, let's consider a person who had done horrible things when they were alive. In the same way, this person will find themselves drowned in the twists and turns of the reality they created. In these two cases, the souls are truly stuck inside illusory worlds that they themselves have constructed.

All of the mediums have told us this in various ways, and this seems to be an inescapable point in the process whenever the recently deceased person hadn't been prepared: the soul is stuck on the earthly plane. Some do not even realize they have died, and return to their homes as if nothing had happened. Loan knew a lady who lived this way with her dead husband for five years. She felt his presence every day: he would sit beside her on the couch to watch television and would lie on the bed during the night. Their life as a couple almost hadn't changed. This did not bother the lady. On the contrary, she appreciated her husband's presence.

Other souls may also be shocked and remain frozen at the site of an accident, for example. They are planted there, outside of time and space, without the ability to move. Here, again, assistance is necessary for their evolution. As I have said, having spent one's life thinking that there is nothing after death blocks many souls who, once they are on the other side, are completely lost because what they are experiencing does not correspond at all to their convictions. Conversely, others are so crippled by the notion of hell that they would prefer not to move rather than risk falling into it.

Once the soul has accepted the fact that it has left its body and is continuing its voyage into the beyond, it passes through the tunnel of light that is so often described during testimonies of near-death experiences. Beings who were dear to them in this life and in their earlier lives welcome them, along with beings of light that are also called "guides" or "angels." It is then time for the soul's evolution. It sees the film of its life play out before it. It often sees it several times, in slow motion and with a few rewinds, so that as much can be learned from it as possible. It analyzes each event while it is helped and guided by the luminous beings. This is an extremely important step and determines what comes next.

If the soul is damaged, it goes into what Loan calls a "soul convalescent home," a space that mediums each refer to in a different way, even though they are all in agreement about the existence of this transition zone. In this dimension, which to us as incarnated beings appears virtually invisible, the soul will find the care necessary for its reestablishment, which will allow it to continue its progression into better conditions. If details of its life are still demanding to be sorted out, it will remain on the earthly plane to do so, with regular trips to more subtle planes to understand that it is advancing and to benefit from precious assistance. This is very frequently the case. Many souls return close to their loved ones to make up for their failures and repair their errors as much as they can in their new situation. Finally, if the soul has liberated itself and is ready for going up, it will instantaneously leave for evolution planes known as planes "of light." These planes vibrate at frequencies removed from our earthly reality, and the higher they are, the more difficult it is for mediums to access them.

What really stands out about all of this is that the soul has the choice between reincarnating itself on earth (or elsewhere) or continuing its voyage in a subtle way, knowing that this choice is determined by its state of progression. The earth, planet of manifestation in matter, offers plenty of ways to learn and improve oneself. And it's not until after having fully acquired all of these lessons that it is possible to continue to the next stage. A soul may then become a guide for other incarnated beings itself or take on a function within the very complex organization of the invisible.

Getting back to the exact moment when we die, the physical part of our being stops all activity, while the subtle part is put into intense motion. The subtle part readjusts, finds consistency, structures itself, detaches, and modifies its vibrations so that it can continue evolving in the beyond. This process is natural and can be observed in all living beings. In us humans, Loan has noticed that the energy coming out of chakras (channels of communication between the physical body and the environment that are shaped like cones, situated on seven central points between the perineum and the top of the head) is condensed in order to return to the inside of the body.

In this way, chakras close one after another, beginning with the lowest. The seventh remains open, though, because it is through it that the whole group will leave. The subtle planes of the aura accompany this process. The whole thing then forms a huge mass of energy at the head and above it, then escapes and passes onto another plane of existence.

Sometimes the process may take its time and occur before the death. When a person is near death, whether due to illness or old age, they present this same configuration and have one foot in each world. They come and go between the two realities. It is therefore not rare to have a sense of their presence even while they are in their bed several miles away, just as Christelle told us so much about and to which a large number of nursing personnel caring for patients at the end of their lives can testify.[16]

If death settles gradually into a person's life, that person has time to prepare, to accept it, and to know what is coming. On the other hand, if it occurs in a brutal way, there is a

---

16 On this subject see chapter 3 of Stéphane Allix and Paul Bernstein (eds.), *Expériences extraordinaires. Le manuel clinique*, Dunod/InterEditions, 2013.

strong risk that the person will not understand. The person is not ready, they were right in the middle of life, and this sudden change seems impossible to them. They are then paralyzed by the shock, then in denial or rejection. The opening of the consciousness that an intentional spiritual walk can shape during the course of one's existence, in addition to being regularly connected to subtle spheres of light, whatever one's religion or belief, can allow a more direct and peaceful comprehension of the process of transformation that is death.

But in our Western society, death is enemy number one. We have become attached to fighting against it by any means possible. The collective unconscious is stamped with this attitude and influences all of us. Rather than trying to inform ourselves on the subject of death, many among us would rather contend with it, reject it, or act as though it doesn't exist. This is truly a shame, because in behaving this way, we are cutting off a part of ourselves.

Death is a part of all of us. Our body is programmed to die. It follows a natural cycle that the harmony on earth depends on. Let's imagine a little bit what the planet would be like without death: what chaos! Death is part of life; it is one of its necessary and healthy components. But it genuinely is the death of our material vehicle. Our soul continues its journey. Life continues, but in another form.

Family members and friends who have already died are the beings most often designated to welcome the deceased and reassure them about what lies ahead. When she accompanies people near the end of life, Loan has observed, like Christelle, this tunnel of light, out of which emerge loved ones in the form of silhouettes, sometimes with a much younger appearance. A feeling of joy and immense love emanates from them.

When I ask Loan about what the appearance of the beyond might be, I am very surprised by the intimate revelation she makes to me. She has, in fact, two different points of view on this question. One is fed by her experience accompanying others at the end of life, the moment when her perceptions allow her to observe everything that is happening to a person passing to the other side. The other is taken from her own journey, after she herself had a near-death experience following a suicide attempt.

When she is simply an observer, she sees a multitude of subtle dimensions with a variety of densities, colors, and appearances in the immensity and richness of the invisible. All of this is shown depending on spectrums of frequencies that may resonate and that commingle and create different realities.

Her personal feeling is something entirely different. During her near-death experience, she had been immediately taken into the care of beings of light and the range of her choices was very limited. She remembers arriving in a dark and thick space. She was weightless. Around her were standing silhouettes in blue and violet tones. She felt safe and surrounded by kindness. She conversed for a long time with these silhouettes, then they asked her to go back down, to go back into her body on earth. She refused. She no longer wanted to return to her life of suffering; it was impossible for her to go back. So she negotiated. And it wasn't until after finding an arrangement that she finally agreed to continue her life here.

This experience radically transformed her existence. Since then, the beyond has been an integral part of her life. Not only the beyond "after death," but the infinite number of manifestations of the invisible.

Hoping to make up for my recklessness from the beginning of the séance when I told Loan too abruptly that I was expecting something specific from my father, which had the effect of blocking her connection because of stress, I make a last-ditch effort. Even if it stresses her even more, I am going to reveal to her the exact objective of this séance. My hope is that right after my question, in a fraction of a second of relaxation, my father will be able to short-circuit Loan's apprehension and transmit the information to her in the blink of an eye.

I go for it: "OK . . . Papa, can you tell Loan what I put in the casket?"

"He's laughing, telling me, 'You like playing guessing games?' He sure likes to laugh."

"Yes."

"I see a watch and a pair of glasses. There's something that makes me think about dried flowers, or . . . I don't know what it is."

"Can you describe what you're seeing?"

"Some kind of plant, but dry . . . I also see fabric. Is it a fabric that means something? Will you tell me, will you validate or no?"

"Yes, yes."

"I also see a pen, a nice pen. He was in writing at a professional level? It's like the pen represented a gift he might have had."

"Yes, he wrote . . . Well, I called him 'Papa' so now you know that it's my father."

"I was already wondering that."

"Oh really? Why?"

"In the energy, but I wasn't sure. You see, it's that element of doubt that made me unsure, but there's something familiar in the energy between the two of you."

As far as the information being transmitted in the blink of an eye, we're far from that. What's happening? Did my father leave? Does she still have contact, or has her imagination taken over?

"So now, in the details you gave me, how did you perceive them?"

"Through images. I'm a pretty visual person, actually."

"But then how do you know that it's a deceased person sending them to you and not an extrasensory expression? Or something in your imagination?"

"Because he's here. I sense his presence as if he were an incarnated person. It's not just . . . how can I say it, it's not just a vapor with no personality, it's not something neutral. I really feel a personality, a way of being. It's subtle and not easy to describe, but I feel the deceased person's desire to communicate. Their desire to participate, to share a testimony, is what pushes me to say things."

"And now, what is my father pushing you to say?"

"He is very amused by the situation."

"How does he see his role in what we're trying to do?"

"The evidence is what's important in his eyes. To testify that there is something on the other side. He's also talking about the nature of man . . . I'm trying to really listen to him, to not transform what he's saying; he's talking about the importance of appreciating the fact that man is not limited to what he may believe is true, that he is much more complex and rich than he thinks."

"Was it a surprise to him to discover this?"

"Yes, definitely. At the same time there's a kind of relief in him, a kind of liberation. He's an emotional person . . . He's a seeker, he likes to discover and understand things. And finding himself faced with this immensity fills him with great enthusiasm. His path on the other side has only begun, he's at the beginning."

"If he remembers, could he describe the moment of his death?"

"I'm still fixated on this pressure in the chest: 'I can't

breathe anymore, I'm blocked,' and at the same time there's the heart giving out . . . Then it's a surprise, because he hadn't at all finished on earth. He still had the desire to accomplish things, he's saying: 'I was taken off guard' . . . and apparently it has to do with his wife, so your mom. He even feels guilty and would like to ask her to forgive him. He couldn't go to the end of the journey with your mom."

It seems that the connection has been reestablished. Everything that Loan has just said is accurate. My father didn't know how to talk with his wife about what was going to happen. He had mentioned to me several times the fact that he was anxious about leaving her alone.

"Does he remember the moment of the passing?"

"First there's a general sense of panic: 'What's happening?' Panic because of his inability to have control over his body. Because he was a very intellectual man, very strong-minded. He was used to having some sort of mental control. And now, he can no longer control his body at all, general panic . . . Then in the end, it all went pretty quickly. He's making me feel that everything became *vaporous*, like little clouds . . . a weightlessness. This feeling of lightness, weightlessness, was gradual. I see him peeling away from his body and looking down at himself from the outside while his body struggles more and more to breathe. But he's no longer inside, he's already a spectator watching what's happening, and he understands that it's over. But he still stays near his body; I see him . . . he watches himself die . . . It's impressive. He's watching himself die and I can sense he's relatively calm. He understands what's happening, that he can no longer do anything, that he no longer has control. I see people coming around him to help him. He can't do anything else, he's no longer able to speak. And now the body lets go. He stays close by, he doesn't leave right away. In fact, he will be present for the whole preparation of the body, for the ceremony, and even afterwards. He says, 'I didn't leave, I took my time to leave, I couldn't abandon my family like that, too painful . . . I stayed for a while before realizing that my place was no longer on earth and that it was time for me to pass on to something else.' He didn't leave right away, in fact."

"This is really astonishing. I have the feeling that we are communicating and at the same time there's this distance that I sense through his responses, like he isn't the same person."

"That's exactly right. He has disidentified from the person you knew and he has found his essence. He is now living in his essence, which is far vaster than that of an incarnated person on earth. There are still personality traits that are there, or else he's just playing along and taking them up again to make himself recognized."

"Really?"

"Yes, but like you said, he is somewhere else, he's continuing his path, he's moved onto something else."

"He's telling you that he stayed near his body after the death and during the funeral, so he saw very clearly what I put in the casket, right?"

"He's saying, 'Yes.'"

"And what's he sending you?"

"I see another thing, like a little chiffon doll, a little doll from South America, I don't know why."

"I can't give you any feedback for now."

"A very basic little doll. There are colors, colorful fabric . . . These are images coming down all at once onto my internal screen. It may be symbolic, yeah, sometimes we can't take the images I'm seeing for what they are but as symbols."

"Is he showing himself, in his casket?"

"When I'm with him in front of his casket, I can feel he's irritated, very angry."

"Why?"

"I have the sense that things did not go the way he would have wanted . . . I hear him saying: 'Simple, something simple.' He's irritated . . . we're going to cross over this emotion to move onto the rest . . . and then there's this anger about not having done everything he would have liked to do on earth. We're going to go back to the casket."

Is he not more likely to be angry about not being able to show Loan the nature of the objects I hid in his casket? When Loan repeated that my father was saying, "Simple, something simple," I really had the feeling he was talking to her to tell her, "For heaven's sakes, it's simple, something simple!" Hint: "What I'm sending you, why can't you see it? It's something so simple!" My interpretation is completely subjective, but so what? It could still be accurate, since the beginning of the séance with Loan convinced me of the strength of the connection she has established with my father. And for some time now, her own emotions have been distorting everything she receives.

"I'm trying to really understand: when we're spontaneous, when you have no expectation, the information comes and is very accurate, but as soon as I ask a question, it seems like everything starts going haywire."

"Yes, that's it. I see things but it no longer makes sense."

"As if your imagination were mixing it up with other things?"

"Yes, I think so, everything is mixing together. And what we need to know is that when the deceased have passed through different stages, they forget, too. Meaning that what is material is swept away. It no longer holds any interest for them."

"Yes, but he knows, and he confirmed this to you, that one of the important parts of these séances is giving the responses I'm waiting for."

"I'll get there eventually. I see lots of things but it's all going in different directions."

No, she will not get there eventually. Despite a connection that is obviously very strong and quite convincing at the beginning of the séance, Loan will be unable to unequivocally give me the names of any of the objects.

Nevertheless, I have learned a lot from this séance with her. In addition to sharing her barely believable journey and the universe that she allowed me to discover, the test part, which we end on a slightly disappointed note, remains rich with teachings. This test supplements the others, in particular the one I had with Christelle. It demonstrates the decisive significance of the emotional factor in a séance with a medium. We will have to remember this piece of information and take it into account if we would like to better comprehend the possibilities and limits of this practice.

Asking a question may expose you to receiving an answer that may not necessarily be correct.

Florence

Florence Hubert was the very first medium I met, nearly ten years ago. That day, I discovered what was involved in a public séance with a medium. It was also a beginning for her, as she had at that time just barely entered the profession. Sitting in a room with several hundred people, I was surprised to see that she and the other mediums present seemed to see the deceased among us, and that the details they were giving were often correct. This made the experience very emotional for the people who recognized a deceased child or parent.

My brother Thomas had died a few years before and I was holding onto the hope that he would show up, so when Florence called out to me from the stage to say that she could see a deceased person standing next to me, I was stunned and quite curious about what she was getting ready to tell me. Unfortunately, the organizer of the event interrupted her because he was behind in his program, and I never got to hear the end of the story.

Since then, I have had the chance to work with Florence on a number of occasions and have noticed the precision and power of her abilities as a medium. I have observed that she usually is able to manage her emotions very well, even if she remains susceptible to them, like anyone with these particular sensitivities. This is not so much the case in private or public séances as it is in tests like the one we are going to conduct today. She has actually taken part in a number of experiments with me in a variety of contexts, and the results were astounding at several moments.

In spite of all of this I am worried. I have seen that even though the previous séances were performed in an atmosphere of mutual trust, the fear of not succeeding was their principal handicap, regardless of their abilities as mediums.

I know now just how difficult it is for a medium to be transparent, how difficult it is to be in a state of perception that is totally untouched by personal psychological influences. I also know that on the other side, it is clearly not a simple task to sync with my expectations, and that my priorities are not necessarily those of the deceased, my father in particular.

I nevertheless decide to begin the séance as I did with the others, without giving Florence any guidance, without even showing her the photo right away. This way, by asking her to capture everything that comes to the surface, I am taking the risk of seeing other people emerge who cannot be identified, and as a result losing time and energy before arriving at my father. But I sense what Florence is capable of, and I would like to understand what drives the arrival of one deceased person versus another.

Curiously, Vadim is the one who shows up first, a young Frenchman who died in the same accident that took my brother.[17] Florence gives me several details that very quickly lead me to realize that it's definitely him she's describing, most notably a few particularities that I have never talked about. Why is he coming? Hearing what he expresses through Florence,

---

17 Stéphane Allix, *La mort n'est pas une terre étrangère*, Albin Michel, 2011, J'ai Lu, 2014.

he seems most of all to want to tell me that he's doing well, that he has passed over just fine to the other side and that he didn't suffer. He appears joyful to Florence, who tells me she sees him crinkling his eyes, laughing. I do indeed have this memory of him; Vadim usually had a mischievous and laughing gaze, with almond eyes behind which a great sensitivity and intelligence could be seen. This encounter is unexpected and moving. It lasts around ten minutes, in a fairly clear and direct manner, no hesitation, then another person suddenly intervenes. Florence has no photo, remember.

"Your father is deceased?"

"Yes."

"Was he fully rational?"

"I'm going to tell you as little as possible."

"Ah, okay . . . I have a man who's a bit confused, my head is spinning. I also have a lot of love to give that he may not have known how to communicate. I have the number two in connection with him. Do you still have a brother?"

"Yes."

"There were three of you? So two who are still here and one who left, is that right?"

"Yes."

"It's like he's drawing an 'L' for me, or the beginning of an 'I' . . . What is this man's name?"

"If you don't mind, I'd rather not say."

"Okay . . . um, the 'L' . . . maybe Louis . . ."

"Louis? That was his father's name."

"He has found Louis."

With no guidance, it seems fairly obvious that it's my father who Florence is picking up on: "a man who's not entirely rational," that was the case for him at the end of his life; a communication problem related to love, yes, as we've seen; and Louis. For a first name that was given so quickly, and for

187

it to happen to be my grandfather's, we have to admit that would be a hell of a coincidence. My father has shown up spontaneously, then, without needing me to show his photo. And Florence instantly identified him as my father. This is off to a good start.

"I have someone with a strong personality, his choices needed to be respected. How long has it been since he left?"

"A year and a half."

"You look like him . . . oh yes, I see his face. He has no regrets about his earthly journey, but he does have some about the end of his life. There's something he's having a hard time absorbing. Was he afraid of dying? I sense this apprehension . . . I'm getting deep breaths . . . He left at the hospital?"

"Yes."

Florence inhaled forcefully as she asked her last question. We might say about just about anybody that "he was afraid of dying" without risking making a mistake, but she is also mentioning the respiratory problems that my father had.

"He's an introverted man, he has a hard time expressing his feelings. He's asking to be forgiven for not knowing how to explain things. He's someone who really likes being outside, greenery, he really likes a house with a space in front of it . . . Did your father sometimes have moments of distress? Moments of loneliness?"

"Yes."

"He's telling me, 'You see an oyster? It closes itself.' Voilà, that's him: he closes himself and doesn't do what he should with other people."

Florence is obviously certain that she is communicating with my father. At no moment have I confirmed this, however. I recognize her assurance when her perceptions are very strong. She has mentioned in particular the resemblance she sees between us. What she says next is exactly in line with his personality: an introverted man, closed like an oyster whenever it came to expressing his feelings. What she said about his love for nature is also exactly right, about that house with an outdoor space . . . We are undoubtedly with him. I decide to take out the photo. She looks at it.

"That's definitely who I'm seeing . . . I have him younger, that's why you look like him. Your father didn't drink, did he?"

"Yes, he did."

I feel like Florence was annoyed to ask me that. I answered in the affirmative without giving any more details.

"He's titillating me a little with bottles. I don't know what he's looking for inside but he goes looking for it now and then . . . The bottles, let's put them behind us . . . I have a regret and an apology to give you, and probably to the rest of the family, too."

Alcohol was not, strictly speaking, a problem for my father, but it was present in his daily life. Never one meal without red wine, midday or evening. Plus aperitifs. It was to the point that during his final years, his alcohol consumption had impacted his health. My brother and I managed to pull ourselves out of this destructive psychological dependence through a sustained effort.

When reality frightens us or causes us to despair, alcohol is the ideal and legal means to no longer look it in the face. In a world where it's hard to find one's place, it offers a space of rest, however temporary and illusory, that is very much welcomed. It allows us to press "pause" when we no longer have the will to try and understand our fears, when everything is too hard, too uncomfortable. Alcohol authorizes this gentle escape, this tender letting go of responsibility. Why should we look ourselves in the face when we can easily put that off until tomorrow? The problem quickly becomes insurmountable, because tomorrow is always tomorrow.

In people who consume a great deal of it, as was the case in our family, alcohol also testifies to an irrepressible desire to take part in a spiritual journey . . . a journey we have not yet found the entrance to.

So we wear ourselves out, we go into a decline, we have less and less courage to do anything differently, and energy abandons us. Alcohol is a permanent death. It's a trap. A terrible trap. It does not allow one to pass on to something else the way that death does; it freezes everything. It freezes life, love, energy, courage. It closes us inside an anesthetizing spiral where, in the end, life flows by, we grow old, and we realize, often at the last minute, that we have passed it by.

The solution is simple, though: stop. Understand that the rigorous discipline that abstinence requires makes us free and alive in each moment. Soon we see revealed to us what has remained invisible up to now: the answers.

Life takes on all of its meaning when we fashion it for ourselves.

The meaning of life does not fall straight from the sky.

No one gives it to us. Not God, not Buddha, nor any other human being. No one but ourselves.

But here we are touching on one of the essential problems of our era, one that manages to make us believe that professional, personal, and even spiritual fulfillment comes via a comfortable and entertaining path. So we are trained in this race of consumption, of forgetting, and even spirituality becomes a product rather than a path of effort and questioning. Liberty, light, and the meaning of existence are not acquired by protecting ourselves from the world, but by looking it in the face every second with confidence and hope. This means shining a light into each dark zone that we might experience. But no, we would rather camouflage it and change nothing: when things don't work well, we tell ourselves that it could be worse, and so we do nothing. We have a hell of a time on the weekend, we party, we enjoy ourselves. And life goes by this way.

Fortunately, in the end, death delivers us from our cowardice or our apprehension and offers us the chance to occasionally become who we are.

Alcohol probably protected my father, but it also distanced him from a certain kind of inner peace. This became very clear to him after his death.

We are all mediums. Each one of us possesses this ability to perceive what remains inaccessible to our other senses. In many people this aptitude is embryonic and will never be expressed. It may even be repressed. In other people it will become too invasive, even uncontrollable, to the point that it drives them to the brink of insanity. And then certain other people will manage to develop it, to nourish it, to understand it, and will do astounding things with it, like the mediums I have met throughout this book. Like Florence Hubert. Yes, without contest, this human being is equipped for perceiving the subtle and invisible world populated by spirits, guides, and the energy of the deceased that surrounds us and is an integral part of our reality.

As far back as she can remember in her childhood, Florence always had flashes, moments when she was struck by an intuition and also heard voices. Before becoming an adult, she had a complicated relationship with these perceptions. While first the object of small frights mixed with curiosity, they would be the cause of significant rejection and suffering during her adolescence. The solution comes when she is older: close herself off, refuse to give access, and live a normal life as a married woman, a comfortable life with children, a house, vacations in Corsica, a beautiful car, etc. But beneath the chrysalis of appearances, her being is cramped. And it is at the doors of death, at the age of forty, that Florence realizes that she cannot flee forever from who she really is. This revelation will be violent.

When she is a little girl, Florence regularly hears murmuring and voices calling to her. Her brother, who is three years older than her, also "sees things." But the children are not able to put it into words. They talk about it very little; the adults always say that it's their imagination. The religious education they receive at school talks about heaven, hell, and purgatory. What if they're seeing and hearing ghosts? Then fear takes over because ghosts "are scary."

But Florence doesn't see anything, at least not right away. She says that began when she started feeling presences. With time, she did start seeing shadows, feeling someone caressing her hair, a light touch. Voices continued calling to her: "Florence." She doesn't know where they're coming from or why. At school, the rare occasions when she tries to talk about it unleash the teasing and jokes of her classmates.

So she decides to handle all of this on her own.

Well . . . not completely on her own.

Even if Florence is independent and resourceful very early on, ever since she was born, she has always had a strong ally on her side: her guide. A guide who entered her life in the most peculiar of ways.

When I ask her how this meeting happened, Florence hesitates, then stands up. "I'm going to show you my friend but don't make fun of me, okay?" She pulls an old yellow stuffed animal out of a box and says to me: "Here's my bosom buddy." She explains to me that she had this stuffed animal in the shape of a cat when she was born, and that she always talked to it as a child. I don't understand, and I tell her this. She tells me that when she would pick up on a presence or hear something that frightened her, she would take this stuffed animal in her arms and tell it about what was happening. The strange thing, though at the time it was perfectly natural to the little girl, is that when Florence would ask it something, the stuffed animal would give her an answer inside her head. This little cloth toy was, in a way, a connecting thread for her relationship with her guide. Florence never left the toy. Every night the little yellow cat would sleep with her and Florence would speak to it the way she would to a confidante. Every time, she would continue asking it questions and continue receiving answers. The questions may have been about friends or any other subject.

Today, Florence has known for a long time that stuffed animals can't talk, and explains that the object served as an agreement between herself and the guide, whose identity she did not discover until much later.

At first, this happens completely unconsciously: it's just a little girl talking to her toy. The fact that the toy responds is not abnormal for a child. As she gets older, she realizes that another reality is taking shape. She hears a voice, but in her head, it's not her own. This is the first time someone has told me that a guide used a stuffed animal to open a dialogue with a person. Who would have thought?

Now, the stuffed animal is carefully stored in a box. Florence no longer needs it because she knows how her relationship with her guide functions. The stuffed animal nevertheless served as an intermediary for over twenty years. Indeed, she didn't put it away in its box until after her first daughter was born.

So many times, Florence had heard her mother ask her, "Who are you talking to?" because her dialogue with the invisible, and especially with her guide, had always been such an important part of her life. She has a sort of angel, a protector she cannot see but who always gives her advice. He protects her, distancing her from certain people who could hurt her. At school, for example, his voice would warn her against a relationship that might be a little complicated and harm the sensitive child that she was. It was an invaluable protection, she believes today. "I wouldn't give it away for two barrels of laundry detergent, that's for sure," she says, laughing.

Florence remains a solitary child. In puberty, she becomes a tomboy. She is more and more uncomfortable with other people and prefers to keep herself at a distance. At the age when most people are constructing themselves, she has more of an impression that she is demolishing herself. Only dance, which she practices often, provides a kind of social life for her. But when her friends go out, having fun and primping themselves, Florence stays in a corner, keeps her hair cut short, and wears jeans, baggy T-shirts with no shape, and clogs. This imprisonment will go on for two years. Even if she doesn't show anything, she is considered to be bizarre, and solitude seems to be the only solution to protect herself from ridicule.

When she enters high school, after having been made very weak because of her difference, Florence decides to blend in at all costs. She no longer feels like living the way she's been living. She wants to have fun with friends and no longer hear comments about how she's always off to the side. But since the perceptions are still there, and because she doesn't know how to stop them or how to no longer hear the voice of her guide, she decides to do exactly the opposite of what the voice recommends. This will not happen without causing her a few problems. The barriers drop, and hanging out with the wrong people follows. Between the mistakes of a teenager, poor choices, and a sensitivity she cannot shake, Florence goes from one extreme to the other. It goes too far. The police make a few visits to the house. Frustration.

As she progresses through adolescence, Florence is constantly living on the razor's edge between the material world and the spiritual universe, within which she knows things exist, even if she does not understand what they are. "You're not crazy, Florence, but don't talk about it, and live with it in silence," she ends up telling herself. And that's what she does.

As much as her dialogue with a stuffed animal had been reassuring and constructive in her childhood, when she gets married and becomes a mother, she wants to understand where this voice is coming from. She then needs to put this part of herself and her life into words. So she asks, and one fine day she has an experience that will mark her for the rest of her life: her guide appears to her.

This happens in the middle of the night. It's like a discharge of unconditional love, an event outside of any control, a sensation coming from outside herself. Florence feels terribly good, she is overwhelmed, and she hears the voice that is so familiar reveal its first name. Everything in her understands what is happening and the significance of it. This is her guide; she knows it. This is not her imagining what she's feeling in this moment. She experiences the power of a connection with a superior master. It's more powerful than she is, it crosses through her, and she is submerged in a swell of happiness. At the time, she hadn't read anything about guides or anything of the sort. She doesn't even use the word "guide," but calls him "my friend."

Florence has just turned twenty and had a baby. She reveals nothing about this part of herself to her husband. He wouldn't understand it. This is hard for her. A car accident will signal the end of this relationship, an emotional shock that leads to divorce. What is most interesting is that today this man is not only aware of what his ex-wife does, but they are now on very good terms and he even sometimes comes to her for consultations.

Since her adolescent years, Florence has talked about these things with her mother, which helps her a great deal. A little over a year after the overwhelming encounter with her guide, it is thanks to her mom that another important event will take place during an interview with a medium in Nantes.

As Florence enters the medium's office, the woman stares at her and says straight out, "I'm happy to see you, Florence," adding that her guide was waiting for her and had told the woman his name. It's the same name he had murmured to Florence on that very intense night. This confirmation is a shock. The medium continues her revelations and Florence hears things she has foreseen for a long time—for example, the fact that she and her guide had been twin brothers in a former life, something Florence had told her mother intuitively years before.

This woman will do a great deal to help Florence find herself again, to reassure herself, to better understand what she is receiving from the invisible, and to finally be able to put the world of the beyond into words. She tells Florence that she is going to become a medium, and that her perceptions will develop more and more. Florence is twenty-five at the time.

But shortly afterwards, she meets the man who will become her second husband and she once more dives headfirst into the hypermaterialist world. Once again, she closes everything with a double-lock. Florence is a pharmacy technician then. Two children are born during her second marriage. Something is not in its place in this life, but oh well, her existence is comfortable and the money keeps her from asking herself too many questions.

The medium's predictions ring truer each day: Florence's perceptions are increasing. This becomes invasive, though she doesn't reveal anything about it to her husband. The more time passes, the more Florence feels, sees, and hears. Something is developing in her. This is becoming obvious, but Florence refuses to acknowledge it. The more she pushes back, the more pressing it becomes. Until the explosion on August 25, 2001, the day that Florence dies.

In her apartment north of Toulouse, Florence is sitting across from me. For some time now, she has been in communication with my father. As with the other mediums, he mentions different details about his life and the end of his life. Florence tells me she hears him and that she sees the images he's sending to her.

"I see him sitting down and standing up, and he's no longer trembling in the legs. I feel like he's more solid today, solid in his head."

In his final weeks, my father struggled to walk and we had to help him. The image Florence is presenting to me is clear and accurate.

"The loss of your brother destroyed this man. He's saying that 'it was a great tragedy.' After your brother's death he wasn't the same . . . There are things that must have broken down."

"Yes."

"You have a daughter? Because he's saying, 'For the girl, she's beautiful, she needs to be told that her grandfather is looking after her and that she doesn't need to be afraid'. Is your daughter afraid of her own success?"

"I'll tell her."

"He's saying, 'I'm skipping.' That's what it is, he wasn't walking a lot at the end, was he?"

"No."

"'I'm skipping,' he's telling me. He's happy, he found his son up there. But I'm not getting your brother, today's not the day."

"Can he describe the end of his life? And what happened after?"

"This man is relatively alone at the end of his life. It's strange, or else he lost the thread of his life, or there was something that wasn't making sense to him in his head. He's afraid of going to the other side. Afterwards, it's as if there was a brutal letting go . . . It's weird, I don't know why, but even though he's disconnected from himself at the hospital, he can hear what people are saying. He's saying, no one's saying anything bad, he's happy . . . the 'J' . . . What was your father's name?"

"Jean-Pierre."

"No one's saying anything bad," does that go along with the meticulous care I took not to pronounce a single negative word when I was talking to him in his last moments?

"He's beaming, he's happy to be there, he found friends. You will have to ask your mother, I think it's René, yes, René, a very good friend of his who he found on the other side."

One of his closest friends was named René. Is that who that is? Coincidence? This René had died in a car accident in England.

"Yes, one of his friends was named René," I answer.

"'We're having a debate,' that's what I'm hearing. He's an intelligent person, he doesn't like to be disturbed, that's important to him . . . Did you tell him goodbye?"

"Yes."

"He's saying, 'I would have liked to tell you goodbye again, goodbye.' I don't know what your relationship was like with him but he's someone who had a hard time expressing himself, that's obvious. He would have liked to say quite a few things again, but he adds, 'You shouldn't feel guilty.' This is strange . . . 'For me, it was written like that . . . I had the hope of finding my son.' He wanted to find your brother, he was hopeful he would see him again . . . The month of June is significant for this man."

"He died in June."

I can still remember very clearly our last goodbye. It was Friday night, and he would die on Sunday afternoon. What was strange was that day I made the round-trip journey from Paris just to spend a few minutes with him. It had been decided that my mother would spend the night at his side so I could spare myself the ninety-mile drive. All three of us were exhausted by our turns watching over Papa, but it was somehow clear that I had to go see him that night, and I took to the road without thinking.

I found him alone in his bedroom. We had talked a little bit. He hadn't eaten; he was sometimes a little confused, trying to uncap or unscrew his water glass as if there were an invisible lid on it, asking me to put water in his red cabbage salad to season it. He realized it was absurd but on the whole things were all right. We talked about literature a little bit, and I asked him what the most significant book or books were in his eyes. I already knew the answer. He listed three, "two of which are inaccessible because their texts are unparalleled," he told me: *War and Peace* and *The Charterhouse of Parma*, and the third . . . *The Tartar Steppe*.

Around 8 p.m., after reminding him that I would be back the next day and that I would spend the following night with him, I told him goodbye and went into the hallway. But after a few yards I hesitated, as if a force was commanding me to stay longer. My mother would be there soon, there was no reason for me to be worried, but I turned around and retraced my steps. I still have a distinct memory of this hesitation, this power that made me go back into the room. I opened the door; he was sitting on the edge of his bed, just as I had left him. My hand on the doorknob, our eyes meeting, I asked him if he was sure that I could go. He answered, "Yes." And that was our last exchange. "Yes, it's fine, go ahead." He was looking toward me and looking at me with great emotion, then he turned toward the window, contemplating the sky that was starting to turn pink, the hand on the clock tower of the church in Nemours, the darkness slowly moving in. So I went back out and started going down the long hallway again, walking very slowly. As if the hospital hallway was enormous and endless. I felt magnetized, having to fight against an invisible bond that kept me held to my father. I couldn't leave.

That image of Papa looking out the window into the ending day is the last image I have of him when he was conscious. He was already drifting a little bit, confused, between two worlds.

We had said our goodbyes, but I imagine he probably wanted to tell me many other things.

He probably didn't have the words. And besides, what to say?

I am happy we exchanged that last look. He was handsome and fragile at the same time. Intense and transient all at once. Nothing required me to go to the hospital that Friday evening, and yet I did. Consciously, the future was indefinite, but a part of me knew. This was why I got in my car, this was why I turned around in the hallway.

The next morning he had a final aspiration of the ascitic fluid. He was still conscious when my mother left him, but he lost consciousness shortly afterwards. At the same moment, I was at home in Paris and I remember feeling heavy, as though I were being sucked to the ground, dreading the night to come. I left for the hospital in the late afternoon. He was unconscious. I didn't realize until later that it was listening to that little voice inside of me that had allowed me to say goodbye to my father.

On August 25, 2001, Florence is in Corsica, in Porto-Vecchio where the family usually spends their vacations. Scuba diving is on the program. The last one of the summer, in a deep spot known for its good-sized grouper. At this time, Florence does a lot of this demanding sport and has achieved a high level of technical skill.

The dinner the night before had been light, and Florence had had a very good evening. On board the boat that takes them to the dive site, she gets ready. The weather is magnificent. Four of them are diving: her husband, two friends, and Florence.

Once they arrive at the site, the four teammates jump into the water and disappear beneath the surface. The bottom remains invisible for the moment, too far away. Florence uses the chain of the anchor to move down. Four yards beneath the surface, as a safety measure, everyone stops and checks that their equipment is working properly. Pressure regulators, tanks, air supply, everything is inspected. Everything is going well. The descent into the crystalline water begins. As they progress, the light wanes, everything becomes uniformly blue, and the water temperature lowers while the pressure increases. The four friends begin to make out the dark mass of the sea floor and soon they are delicately landing on it. They are forty-four yards beneath the surface. At that depth, the jokes are over.

Florence touches down, sending up a cloud of sediment with her palms. Myriad small fish race to swallow up the microorganisms dispersed by the divers. The spectacle is magnificent. One more safety check. The divers look at each other and signal that everything is all right. A flashlight is turned on and makes the colors burst from a depth where the mass of water filters the sun's rays and lets only gray-blue pass through.

The divers begin moving; Florence is at the back of the team, her ex-husband in front of her. The first diver turns toward his friends and signals them that he has just seen a big fish. All of them move to follow him and pause between two enormous rocks. The first diver passes, the second and the third follow, then comes Florence's turn. As she soars through she inhales a new gulp of air, but then she is dumbstruck: it's salt water that has penetrated her pressure regulator.

She instantly has the reflex to pick up a pebble from the ground and hit it against her metal tank to get the attention of the diver in front of her. Her ex-husband turns, and Florence signals that she has no more air by placing her hand horizontally over her throat. He joins her instantly and lands in front of her. She tries to inhale again, but there's only water. Without hesitating, her ex-husband hands her his own mouthpiece while he grabs the other from Florence.

Now there's another big problem: after having activated the valve to expel the water in it and putting it in her mouth, Florence breathes in . . . water.

What is happening? Her ex-husband is now breathing normally with Florence's mouthpiece. Her panic starts to mount. Florence opens her eyes wide, not understanding and not knowing what to do. She makes a sign again to her ex-husband that she still doesn't have air. Out of reflex she lifts her head but the surface is too far away. Above her, she can only make out an infinite mass of water. She knows she will not have the time to make it up. She has to manage to breathe here where she is or she is lost.

Everything happens very quickly.

Her ex-husband gives her his second emergency pressure regulator. It had also been checked before the dive. It works. As her lungs cry out for air and the need for air becomes more and more unbearable, Florence flushes the regulator, places it over her mouth, and breathes . . . water.

At that moment she tells herself she is going to die. She knows she doesn't have enough time to get to the surface. She looks at her ex-husband with panic, then at the invisible surface, returns to the face looking back at her, and everything clashes, everything shoots through her head, panic sets in, all at great speed. In an uncontrollable survival reflex, she inhales . . . and everything stops.

She is dead.

But she sees.

She suddenly finds herself off to one side.

She observes the scene: she's facing her ex-husband, who is holding her by the straps of her suit. The two other divers are there, powerless spectators at the tragedy that is taking place.

She is watching all of this from a distance.

She is to the right of the four divers, watching without understanding, at once detached but profoundly disturbed: "Am I not dead?" This must be a terrible mind game, a dream.

In the same instant a kind of haze arrives on the right side. Florence describes something enormous, extremely bright and gentle. She rushes inside it, without even asking any questions.

She is inside a delicious atmosphere; she is fine, just fine. She feels two arms lifting her up; she's no longer dizzy. Florence is perfectly calm, confident, and very serene. She feels bathed in love. She emerges into a gigantic, bright room that looks as if it is made of light. There is a bench. For a few seconds Florence wonders where she is, and suddenly she sees her guide for the second time in her life.

He is the one who lifted her up; he has let go of her and is now is in front of her. Florence is facing a bench on which three beings—who look like hooded monks—have suddenly appeared. When the one in the middle lifts his head, Florence sees that his eyes are extraordinarily blue. The being asks her, "What do we do with you now?"

Without even thinking, Florence says, "I'm staying." In that moment, nothing else is important. She is the mother of three daughters but she doesn't hesitate a second: "I'm staying here."

The beings tell her, though, that this will not be the case. They show her a sort of panorama, a field of vision where, like in a film, scenes of her life appear. Her childhood, her marriages, the births of her daughters, her brothers, etc. Everything goes very quickly, weaving together, tangling into this enormous ball where all of the images concerning her are projected. When Florence looks at the beings again, the one in the middle tells her, "Now we are going to show you why you came."

But Florence doesn't remember anything about that part. A black hole.

She finds herself suddenly back in her body, which the three drivers are bringing up. She regains consciousness when they are fifteen yards down. Her ex-husband controls the speed of their progression toward the surface, despite the urgency, because it would be suicidal to add a decompression accident to what just happened down below. Florence first hears the sound of bubbles, then realizes she is breathing air again. The mouthpiece has remained in her mouth and is now working. Having fully regained her senses and realizing she is still underwater, Florence doesn't want to remain there one more second. In an uncontrolled reflex, she grabs her pressure regulator and hastily fills her stabilizing jacket, which the other divers had carefully deflated at the bottom. The effect is immediate and she ascends abruptly through the water like a balloon full of air and passes from under fifteen yards to the surface in two seconds.

With exploded eardrums and the right side of her face paralyzed, Florence vomits without being able to stop. The situation is critical. The rescue team arrives quickly and Florence is evacuated by helicopter before being placed in a decompression chamber at the hospital in Ajaccio.

Her loss of consciousness at the bottom prevented her from swallowing seawater and drowning. She had been unconscious for several minutes, during the time of the slow and prudent return to the surface. And in the time outside of time, Florence had made a brief foray into death in what is called a near-death experience.

When she comes out of the chamber, her husband looks at her and says, "I don't recognize you, you don't have the same eyes. You're not my Florence anymore; you're not the same."

She responds, "I guess not. What are we doing together?"

A wake-up call, that's the phrase, in the hospital.

Florence had just celebrated her fortieth birthday two weeks ago.

The most astonishing coincidence is that on that day, on a boat moored not far from the Porto-Vecchio beach, a vacationer observed the whole scene from a distance: the arrival of the ambulance, the helicopter taking off. Unbeknownst to them, this man would become Florence's friend a few years later. His name is Dr. Jean-Jacques Charbonier, the doctor from Toulouse specializing in . . . near-death experiences.

As often happens, even shattering realizations like the one Florence had are not necessarily followed right away by radical life changes. It would take Florence three years to make the decision to leave. But within a few months she meets several mediums who confirm to her that this is the time and that she is capable. So she goes for it. She leaves her husband and her way of life, moves with her daughters into low-income housing, and becomes a medium.

Like Henry Vignaud, she begins with public séances to help her get a leg up. In her case, things are going to happen very quickly.

I am always surprised when mediums talk about public séances. I imagine that finding yourself in front of a large crowd of anxious people for the first time must be terribly unnerving, yet even if before she starts the anxiety can be very strong and sometimes debilitating, once on the stage, Florence, like the others, tells me she feels like she's in another world. She no longer sees the room, nor the people, and she is literally guided.

Sitting at a table on which photos of the deceased have been placed by families and friends who are present, Florence has the feeling of finding herself in a fog, a kind of mist. Something wraps around her. Then, she mechanically grabs a photo and her perceptions open up. She hears voices, people talking to her, describing details of their lives to her, the circumstances of their death, first names or sometimes just the first letter, dates, etc. In this state, whether she is in front of one person or five hundred doesn't change anything. She is plugged into another reality. She is no longer completely herself. She is in front of what resembles a large screen, on which she sees episodes from her own life during her near-death experience. All around her head the images, sounds, and sensations are going by in a great choreographed ballet. Things move, things pass, and then they go. It's a kind of interactive space where she sees the energy of the deceased presenting itself to her and showing her many little details. Sometimes, it starts to evaporate, and Florence realizes that her own spirit is getting the upper hand, a sign that she should stop.

To reach this state, Florence doesn't really meditate, but she asks for authorization by putting herself in connection with her guide. This is the same guide who taught her the little phrases, a few lines each, that she had to recite in these situations in order to open the channel. Today she knows them by heart; they have become automatic.

Florence talks about three kinds of mediumship. What she practices is called "semi-conscious mediumship," but there is also "conscious mediumship," which is similar to "mechanic mediumship," which would correspond to incorporation. In the third case, the medium doesn't remember anything at the end of the séance. Their face may be transformed during the trance by the effect of the deceased soul's penetration of their body. This type of mediumship is apparently dangerous, and very few mediums in the world practice it. In semi-conscious mediumship, which is Florence's kind, she is able to speak to the person who has come to see her and communicate with the deceased. Now the deceased is all she sees. The third form of mediumship, therefore, is seeing, with flashes, static intuitions that are very different from contact with a deceased person, according to all of the mediums I have questioned on this topic.

In private, as for this test today, Florence takes the photo of the deceased in her hands, requests permission, then places the photo back down, turning it over. From the moment the connection begins, she almost no longer needs it. Then, either the energy of the soul of the person in the photo presents itself, or someone else arrives, but in any case, Florence knows that her guide is acting as a filter. He is protecting her, and her client, from possible sources of interference.

These sensations are identical to what she feels in public. She feels embraced, as if she is sheltered beneath a kind of large cape. She is well, it's warm, and she receives the information. When she is completely receptive, she almost doesn't see the person consulting her anymore. But however little that other person speaks to her, it always brings her back down to earth. Then, to reconnect herself again is more difficult. In general, she likes it better if people allow her to speak in the early part of the consultation, and asks people to write down their potential questions for later.

How did Florence learn to trust her feelings? She tells me she feels what she is capturing "in her gut." She knows when she is anchored, balanced, and she discerns internally that what she is perceiving is real. When this sensation of being centered withers, she prefers to stop the séance. In the same way, she has learned to tell the difference between her perceptions and her imagination by observing what she calls "the heaviness of the imagination." By comparison, her perceptions transport her to a state where everything is fluid. The information, the first names, and the dates spurt out in front of her with such clarity. She says out loud, and lightly, what is passing over the screen of her spirit. It flows by itself. Conversely, her imagination requires effort: it gets stuck, it hesitates; in other words, it's not really the same thing.

During a recent public séance, a deceased young boy passes by and says, "Noah." As she asks the people in the room if Noah means something to anyone, two pediatric nurses raise their hands and say that they have just been taking care of a little Noah, who died in their hospital from a brain tumor. The little boy adds that he has come to tell a little girl with an A in her first name that he's waiting for her. The two nurses reveal to the stunned audience that one of their other patients is a little Ambre who is dying. Florence saw this boy and what he said with such transparency, it all came by itself. This spontaneity, the completely unexpected nature of the messages that were emerging, as we have seen, is often an indication for mediums that they are in an authentic perception.

Florence tells me that her guide is filtering what is coming to her from the beyond. I am impressed by this relationship with her guide that is so strong and so present in her life. Who are these guides? Where do they come from? How do we connect to them if we all have them? As far as she is concerned, Florence discovered that she had known hers in a former life. For other people, they may be beings who were never incarnated, who therefore resembled nonmaterial energies. But I retain this one important point from my meeting with Florence: we are not alone; we are never alone. We all have within us a guide who accompanies us from childhood and who will wait for us after death.

For most of us, our guide appears timidly as that small internal voice that we call "intuition." Knowing the name of one's guide, as Florence does, is absolutely not essential for connecting with it. Florence tells me that one must already know how to listen to oneself.

When I ask her how, she suggests I do a simple exercise when I have to make a decision, for example. When we are going to bed at night, even if we don't know who our guide is, we can ask it to answer our question during the night. The next morning the answer is there, accessible to our internal senses. But right away the mind starts working and takes control. So we have to pay attention to this subtle and fragile sensation when we are still in bed, with our eyes still closed, as we are beginning to wake up. That instant right before the dreams dissipate and disappear from our memory. There, in that moment, the answer is breathed to us.

Then, we can no longer prevent ourselves from taking back control. It's our mind, our free will, but intuition, the voice of this guide, must be caught beforehand, in that delicate interstice between sleep and waking.

The doors to the invisible world are more numerous than we can imagine.

Over the course of writing this book, something has become visible to me: the certainty that even if I can't manage to hear him myself, my father is able to talk to me. For some time already I have sensed that it is not impossible for me to one day be able to read the signs of the invisible world. In fact, it has already started.

If we were in need of a final confirmation that everything I have experienced for months with these mediums is truly real, Florence will give it to me. She will pass the test with flying colors, but not before raising a few mysterious points.

"His mother came to look for him. A woman with beautiful eyes . . . Was there a baby that departed from you?"

"Departed? No."

"Who is this little one? There's a tiny little guy . . . He doesn't have a brother who departed?"

"Tell me what's coming to you."

"I have a tiny little munchkin. A year old, a year and a half. He's holding his hand as if he's part of him, part of the family. So is there a baby, a small child who departed? A brother of his? 'Accident,' I'm hearing. 'Accident.' Did this little one drown? I think it's a little boy."

"Who would this child be in relation to him?"

"Someone in the family. An uncle or a brother, but very young."

Florence sees my father holding a child as if it were his little brother, dead in an accident or by drowning. Here is a third mention of this mysterious brother after Pierre and Christelle. It is really profoundly disturbing. I will not, however, receive more information on this subject, so I decide to slowly lead Florence toward the goal we're interested in.

"I'd like to ask him a few things. I'd like him to try and give me details about his last days alive and about what happened next."

"He's drawing me a big 'C,' a first name with a big 'C' who was able to do things for him when he departed, and he's saying, 'You have to go.'"

My mother's name is Claude, but I don't tell Florence this.

"When he left, were you called? Because I'm hearing, 'He has to come . . .' He died when you were there, or you were called because he had just passed?"

"No, I was there."

"You were there . . . Why 'He has to come'?"

"I was already there."

"But were you called to go there?"

"No."

"How is this happening? Because I'm hearing, 'He has to come.' I'm telling you what I'm hearing, so maybe it's not from that day. 'He has to come, he has to be here.' Why is he telling me this? I have no idea."

It's astonishing that despite my denial, Florence is insisting. In general, this means that the deceased person is insisting themselves. Since my father knew I was present, could he be referring to my brother or my mother? Should "He has to come" be understood in the plural? Even though I was alone with him and his breathing had markedly declined, I called my mother and let Simon know. Was he afraid of leaving without their being there?

"He's trembling, he was afraid but he's letting go. After, it happens very quickly, like a relief. And you said to him, after he left: 'Tell me how you're doing, send me a sign.' He heard something like that coming from you . . . He was quite tired on the inside. He was in pain, and I still have something spinning, as if he lost his balance at the end of his life."

"He had weakness in his legs, and he did lose his mind a little."

"He must have been kind, I have a kind energy, but he's also someone who was misunderstood and who didn't know how to express himself. Even with me, he's explaining himself but I have a hard time translating because he's not really used to talking this way."

All of this is very accurate, but I am fixated on Florence's comment, according to which my father is mentioning the fact that I asked him to tell me how he was doing. Is he talking about the test? I'm going to shift into a higher gear and ask Florence the question directly. We're getting close, I can feel it.

"I put things in his casket and I asked him to give me this information through a medium. That's the challenge."

"That's a lot of pressure!"

"No . . ."

"He's been here since this morning. He's getting used to life after life because he didn't really believe in it very much before. He was a little narrow-minded about what we're doing here, but he's telling me, 'Little by little as I've gone further, I'm understanding things, you're helping me . . .' I have something like a pencil, did you put in a pencil? I have a stretched-out shape in his casket, what is it? A pencil?"

"Just tell me what he's telling you."

"It looks like a pencil or a paintbrush, I don't know if that's what it is."

I don't answer, but I acknowledge what Florence says. In spite of the apprehension, she has a clarity of spirit that allows her to obtain very accurate and precise details from the deceased. And what she's just said is indisputable: a long paintbrush; that is exactly one of the four objects I put in the casket. Not a fat one, not a square or a thick one, no, a long and thin paintbrush. I am so overwhelmed. But I don't want to let anything show in front of Florence and I don't react to what she has just said. She continues.

"Voilà . . . and then I have a paper, a little note: 'To my father,' 'For my father,' or 'To my papa,' he has something like that with him."

Remember that with the four objects, I put that note in an envelope in which I told him that I loved him.

"He says he has let go of the old demons, you understand? He may cry because he's sensitive, then he's laughing like crazy. He suffered while he was leaving, he was afraid . . . Did your father paint?"

"Yes."

"Did he paint ocean landscapes?"

"No."

"I'm hearing the numbers fifteen . . . six, sixteen. What day did he die?"

"The sixteenth."

"Ah yes . . . there we go . . . It's like he was pushing something gently in front of me. I'm trying to see, maybe it's a knife; this is strange . . . It's not a paintbrush. I saw the paintbrush earlier. No, this is smaller, did he have a knife?"

"Yes."

He had several, actually, constantly within reach. But I

withhold from saying that this object had not been placed in the casket.

"Okay . . . Who is Paul?"

"I don't know."

"Jean-Paul or Paul?"

"In relation to what?"

"A friend he found."

I don't know why at that moment I say that I don't know. Paul, my father's uncle, who had died, well, *disappeared* during the First World War, has already shown up with two mediums. Here he is again, but I probably am so focused on the test and on the fact that Florence has just passed it that I let Paul slip past me. She senses correctly that he is close to my father. She mentions a friend, but her contact must be very subtle, and without any reaction from me, Florence continues by going back to my father.

"Did he wear a scarf?"

"He liked to, yes."

"I'm seeing him adjusting a scarf so it doesn't hurt his throat."

In the casket, my mother had insisted that we put a scarf around his neck. Reassured by Florence's success, I'm going to continue the séance hoping that my father will talk about the other objects while I ask her about him.

"Does he know he's dead? Did he sometimes have periods of doubt?"

"No, he knows he's dead . . . He's still developing, though. He's seeing people again."

"But as far as my question, are you connected with him right now? Is he present?"

"Yes."

"If you ask him a question, can you get an answer?"

"I don't know, it depends; go ahead, ask."

"If you have him in front of you, why don't you ask him, 'Jean-Pierre, tell me the things that Stéphane put in your casket'?"

"That's going to be a total flop because I'm not getting very much. Did you put in a painting? A drawing? He's showing me a drawing, as if it was something he'd painted. As if he'd taken that famous paintbrush and is starting to paint . . . What I'm seeing now is strange . . . He's taking a painting, then he's painting on it . . . Did you put painting things in; this can't be possible, is that what you put in?"

I don't answer but I observe that for Florence, the presence of the paintbrush is now certain. It's strong.

"Tubes of paint? Yes, that's it! Because in fact he's painting again thanks to you . . . He's repainting," she continues.

"These are images he's sending you?"

"Yes, he's the one sending me the image of himself painting. I can guess that if he's showing me this image, it's because there are things in the casket that allow him to do that. So the paintbrush and the tube of paint. Afterwards, he must have found a canvas on the other side."

This is unbelievable. I am flabbergasted that this is coming so easily. The paintbrush, the tube of paint . . .

"So he didn't say a specific word to you?"

"No."

"He's only sending you images?"

"Yes."

"Do you see other images?"

"After . . . I see . . . It's hard, what you're asking me to do. It's like if I were him, you know?"

"Yes."

"I'm in his place, I'm seeing him paint. I also have a kind of low wall overlooking a valley. I have trees, I don't even know where I am. I see this landscape through his eyes, as if

215

I were in his place. I don't know whether it's a place that he likes very much. Did he live in the country in a similar spot? A small wall, a little nook, and trees in front. It's pretty, calm. He's putting me in front."

"Your description actually resembles the place he was particularly fond of where he lived in the country. A terrace that overhung a little bit, with a little wall that went down."

One of the last pictures I took of my father a few weeks before his death shows him sitting in this spot. His gaze is resting on the tops of the trees that extend all the way to the horizon. He's in his wicker chair, at the edge of the gravel terrace, a terrace that ends with a little overhang that we had built together more than thirty years before. This image is so him. That's the place he wanted to die.

"He just transported me there, without saying a word," Florence tells me.

"I'd like you to describe the perceptions you're getting with as much precision as possible."

"'I'm myself again, in my place. I see the infinity of where I am, and I see all of you, too; I would never have thought this was possible before,' he's saying. 'I'm not impatient, but I know that I will see you again and talk with you again.' Did you see him in a dream?"

"That happens, yes. And actually, in three or four vivid dreams with him, he appeared a little quiet and lost."

"He's putting down roots again. When I tell you that he's in the middle of developing, maybe he shouldn't be asked too many questions, it's better to let him say what he wants to. A year and a half is short. He's still in the process of ascending, of understanding his death. He's on the way. He's a nice man, a beautiful soul . . . He's fine where he is, he's doing better. No more internal suffering. I felt him like someone who was tortured during his earthly period, not comfortable, not expressing himself the way he wanted to, having relational problems with the people around him . . . Where he is now, I sense that he is calm, surrounded by people; there are lots of people with him, he's not all alone."

No, he's not alone. And neither are we. We never are.

Conclusion

As I said before, writing this book changed my life. I had what was perhaps a naive idea about communication with the dead, a number of questions, and many preconceived notions. Working on this book, performing these tests, and spending many hours in ongoing discussion with mediums allowed me to enter into their lives, into the intimacy of their perceptions, and to better understand and sense in myself that access to the invisible world is logically possible.

Beyond the positive and incontestable results of the test— the similarity of the information about my father's life, death, and personality, as well as the mention of deceased members of our family and the countless identical details that each medium provided without fail—together form the proof that my father was never absent during the séances. Each of the six mediums described the same person to me, because that person is alive. The six mediums entered into communication with my father.

My father, like all of the people we love who have left us, is still alive *somewhere else*. The reality is vaster than we are able to imagine. Death does not exist; the bonds of love persist and hold strong.

We are bound to one another forever.

I don't know about you, but this fills me with energy.

Death, the Process of Grief, and Mediumship

A Practical Discussion with Dr. Christophe Fauré

Dr. Christophe Fauré is a psychiatrist specializing in the care of people at the end of life and their loved ones. Today, death has become taboo; we no longer observe traditional mourning periods after the death of a loved one. We live it in silence, imagining ourselves to be strong enough to get through it alone. Most of the time, we are simply unaware of the psychological mechanisms at work in us during these kinds of experiences.

Losing a loved one is traumatic; it is a wound whose repercussions will be felt for the rest of our life. Recognizing this fact is not always easy. How are we supposed to deal with the absence of that person every day? How can we come out of the pathological depictions of grief? How can we break free of our dependency on that link—going to see the grave every day, incessantly consulting mediums, etc.—which can also block our process of grieving? Is the belief in the survival of the soul a significant help during a time of grief? To consult or not to consult a medium? These are the questions we will tackle with this well-known psychiatrist.

Apart from the extraordinary nature of what I have just experienced with these six mediums, and even though today I feel unquestionably in every cell that death is not the end of life, it is still a brutal separation, a moment of unparalleled intensity that intrudes to let a new relationship with the disappeared person emerge. The dead are not dead, but they are no longer present, either. Adherence to the idea of the survival of the consciousness does not diminish the pain and the suffering caused by the absence. Does a medium replace the process of grieving? Can they help? Make it more complicated?

What prompted you to specialize in caring for patients at the end of their lives?
In the eighties, I was a medical student at Necker, and I was doing my rotations as an intern in different surrounding hospitals, one of which was the Pasteur Institute, which at the time had a hospital section with an infectious diseases department. It was the beginning of the AIDS epidemic. There wasn't any AZT yet, and no treatment, and nearly everyone who had it was dying. Many of them were young. This hit me full force. It was a direct, immediate experience. For ten years I volunteered with the non-profit AIDES, and in parallel to that I completed my residency in psychiatry. But my interest already lay in the interaction between psychology, serious illness, and the end of life. I also sensed that I had been very affected by all of those deaths, and that I needed more of a foundation. So I went to the palliative care unit at Paul-Brousse in Villejuif and found Michèle Salamagne, who is one of the pioneers of palliative care in France. She welcomed me warmly and encouraged me a great deal. Little by little, I became one of the team caregivers. After that, we founded the first grief support group.

How would you define the psychiatric approach to the end of life, in terms of how you have developed it?
First we try to isolate the psychiatric manifestations that are linked to the person's physical condition. We examine, based on the different pathologies and treatments given, if what is shown at a psychological level is linked to a psychological state or medical condition.

The second focus of our approach: people who have absolutely no psychiatric history but who will develop panic attacks or episodes of delirium because of the enormity of what is happening to them. They are being confronted by their own finiteness, the loss of control over the things in their life. People become undone psychologically and enter what we call "mental confusion." They completely lose their bearings, no longer recognize their loved ones, and they can no longer distinguish between day and night. It's extremely anxiety producing, as much for them as it is for their loved ones. Elisabeth Kübler-Ross has described very well the depressive movement of life. But some major depression can totally paralyze one's capacity to be in relationships with those closest to them. In that case we're no longer talking about a normal depressive experience at the end of life, but a state of clinical depression. So in those instances, we try to help the person with medical and psychological methods.

Do you sometimes have the impression that the dying person alternates between moments of presence and absence?
I adhere completely to the concept in palliative care according to which the person is present until the final breath— even if they are barely breathing, even if they only have a few minutes left to live, even if they are in a coma that has been

going on for days. Those working in palliative care say hello even when they go into the room of someone in a coma, regardless of whether there had been a prior relationship with that person. We also take a person's arm only after having informed the patient, respecting this principle: "Always say what you are doing first, and then do it." So the person is not afraid. It was Fabienne Chudacet, a doctor at Jeanne-Garnier (Paris) who taught me that. She says, "Madame, I'm going to touch your head, because I need to see how your neck is doing," and then she touches the head. "I'm going to take your hand," and she takes the hand. "I'm going to change your bandage now," etc. There's a principle we follow: beyond what I can see, I know that the person is here, present, living, even if they are not reactive.

What is this principle founded on?
On studies that were done with people coming out of a deep coma. They described their sensations, which allowed them to make a clear distinction between a mechanical touch and a loving touch, to capture the ambiance around them, to experience frustration at not being able to participate in the conversations they heard, etc. On this basis, we adjusted a number of things in our approach to people in comas or who were suffering from altered consciousness.

Have you witnessed any strange phenomena at the moment of death?
One experience in particular really struck me. I was talking with a woman near the end of her life. She was tired but completely in her right mind. I was sitting on her bed, and she was sitting facing me. She was telling me she was worried

about her loved ones. It was a fairly standard discussion. And at the end of the conversation, she asks me, "Listen, do you think I'm lucid?"

"Yes."

"I'm not crazy, right?"

"No, not at all!"

"Well, I have to tell you something: I see my husband, he's at the foot of the bed, right there." And she points her finger in that direction.

I turn to look around, and I say, "Okay. But I don't see him." It's important to be clear about where you stand: we don't recommend going in the direction of something that's not your own reality. But since in this line of work we're used to these kinds of experiences, I ask her, "How does he seem? Is he talking to you, is he saying something to you?"

"It's a little vague; he's not talking, he's just there, as if he were waiting for me."

"Does that worry you?"

"No, no, not at all!" She was very calm; she simply wanted to tell me that this presence was there.

She died two or three days later.

Are those kinds of events frequent?

Frequent and typical, because she was a person who was really very conscious. I was having a conversation with her, and there was no sign of mental confusion in the medical sense of the term. We see quite a lot of disturbing things. For example, another caregiver told me this: a body had been brought to the morgue, and a little later he must have gone back there and he saw a kind of halo of light, like smoke dissipating around the person. Now here's another observation: people say things at the end of life that involve deceased loved ones who come into contact one way or another with them. These experiences almost always bring with them a sort of solace, a certainty. "Someone's coming to get me." However, in my experience, the majority of people do not go through this, but it could also be that many of them experience it without talking about it, or else they are so used to that kind of contact that they don't even think something out of the ordinary is happening. I don't know exactly what takes place, but one thing is certain: these phenomena are described over and over.

Why is it that despite the testimony of people like yourself who have daily encounters with these kinds of phenomena, we are still in denial that these experiences are real?
We are in a society where the irrational doesn't get good press. All of the people who try and reassure themselves that they are normal are quick to affirm just how "Cartesian" they are! As if it were the alpha and the omega of good psychological health to be very logical. So, if we are very logical, everything that cannot be explained is going to be considered fishy, interpretive, neither reliable nor serious. Since we are in a medical context in which we are taking care of people, with procedures, there is perhaps a kind of fear of being labeled "unprofessional," of discrediting yourself by sharing things. The risk of ridicule, of having the quality of your work called into question, generates fears, which sometimes are legitimate because there is also the risk that someone well-versed in this might become proselytizing in their manner of speaking to people near the end of their lives and hammer this discourse into the heads of people who have no desire whatsoever to hear that.

Is there any advice you would give someone caring for a dying person?

There was another experience that affected me when I was younger; it's a story I tell in one of my books.[18] One autumn night at la Salpêtrière, a young boy was dying alone, unconscious, in his room. Outside the patient's room, his family was sitting and waiting. They didn't dare go in. They were afraid; they didn't know what to do. I approached the boy's sister, and we started talking. I asked what she would have needed to tell her brother if he was still conscious right now. Then she talked about her pain, about her regrets, about her love and admiration for him after seeing him show so much courage during his illness. "Why don't you tell him that right now?" I asked her. She looked at me, astonished, and almost shocked that I would suggest that. I talked to her about the significance of those kinds of words. Her parents listened, still silent. Finally she got up and went into the room. She sat down next to her brother and started talking softly into his ear. She raised her eyes toward me just once: "Are you sure he can hear me?" I told her I couldn't be sure, but I thought it was important for her to do it. A few moments later, the mother came in, too, and took her daughter's place to talk to her son one last time. Then it was the father's turn, and then the other brothers'. In the end they were all in the room. They brought in chairs from the resting room and kept watch over their family member all night. They seemed relieved that they had been able to talk to him. He died early in the morning.

Every caregiver in palliative care recommends saying words of love, forgiveness, and gratitude . . . even to people

---

18 Christophe Fauré, *Vivre le deuil au jour le jour*, Albin Michel, 2012.

who are "unconscious" or on the threshold of death. If we weren't able to do it before, when we have the good fortune— and it is good fortune—to be able to care for a dying person (which is different than situations in which death is accidental, violent, or in which we don't have time to say anything), I have the personal conviction that people can hear what is said, even if they are unconscious. And I even believe that it may be important to speak to a person on the verge of taking their last breath.

Do you have other examples that have fueled this conviction?

We've heard so many times about people who were in a coma, who should have died, but who didn't! Caregivers wonder, *What held them back? What wasn't finished? Who is this person waiting for?* I remember very clearly a dying woman whose son was in Australia. He had told her he would be there soon, but something unexpected had happened, problems with the plane, and he was twenty-four hours late. When he came into the room, he said right away, "Maman, I'm here. You can go now, everything's going to be fine, I'm safe, don't worry, you can go if you want to." Fifteen minutes later, she was dead. And that wasn't an isolated case: there are hundreds of stories about people waiting for a word, or the presence of a loved one, and who stay alive as though they were worried that their leaving would be impossible for their spouse or children to bear. So often we hear husbands and wives say something that frees their spouse: "You can go, I'm going to get through this with the kids. We will always love you, but if you want to, you can go now." And afterwards the people would die within an hour, sometimes even in the minutes that followed.

Knowing this, and being able to keep inside the memory of what was said, is very important. Among the people I care for who are in mourning, those who were able to say these kinds of things are relieved. It's as if they had agreed to the departure of their loved one, rather than death having come and taken that person away. And it's very different. Which is why it's important, actually, to be there when it happens. But if we can't be there, what do we do? We may decide to say everything we have to say beforehand, assuming that we may not be present at the moment of death. Of course it's preferable to be there, to be able to say we were with them until the end, but sometimes it's not possible. My advice: say the important things without putting it off until later, because later may be too late.

So, going to see a medium while we are going through grief, is this recommended or not?

First, let's be clear, I never tell my patients to go see a medium. Nevertheless, I notice that people who have lost a loved one sometimes need to see someone who claims to communicate with the beyond. This is true for various reasons. Some are just curious and tell themselves: "I don't believe in it but I want to see." Others have the belief that a life exists after death, so they want to know if the deceased person is doing well, if he's next to them or if he's angry with them, if he forgave them for something that they felt guilty about. Those patients—who, of course, always tell me after the fact that they have seen a medium!—either tell me that the consultation reassured and calmed them or that it did nothing, but at that moment they had needed to go. In any case, even if some people may find relief from it, it will never, in any way—and I insist upon this—shorten the grieving process, which has its own logic.

229

This process is a psychological wound that will scar over time. And in order for that to happen, different stages are necessary. It's not only a question of relieving one's suffering, but also successfully living with the loneliness created by the absence of the loved one, the difficulty of reconnecting socially, the lack of sharing daily life and projects with that person.

When my patients ask me, before doing it, if it's a good idea to see a medium, I tell them that I don't know, and that only they can decide if it's good for them or not. I then invite them to explain their motivation: "Why go see a medium? What are you hoping to get out of it? If there is contact, what impact do you think this might have on you?" I explore their desires and their expectations. Rather than tell them to see or not to see a medium, I only question the grieving person's desire in order to permit them to decide for themselves if this desire is well-founded or if they are expecting unattainable things.

Going to see a medium is going to see someone who claims to communicate with a deceased person. Should doubt always be a part of the consultation?

In my experience, even if not everyone tells me that they are going to see a medium, and apart from cases of addiction, I always observe this protective element of doubt. Yes, doubt is advantageous; it helps a person not adhere blindly to what is said. People often wonder if they had suggested certain answers, or if it's not a little like telepathy. This doubt is a psychological protection from words that are ultimately very arbitrary.

To go into a little more depth, the psychological function of the grieving process is to transform an objective external relationship into an *introjected* relationship with the deceased person. "Introjected" means that the presence of the deceased person becomes internal. When a medium mentions during a séance the persistence of the deceased's consciousness on the outside, for certain people this crystallizes the presence of the deceased beside them. But this presence is artificial. Mind you, I'm not making a judgement about the existence of life after death, that's not what's in question here, but objectively, the deceased is no longer among us in daily life, and keeping that person here by means of repetitive consultations with mediums is also a refusal to accept the reality of their death. This mechanism will work against introjection, which is the normal progression of the grieving process.

I will say this again: I am not voicing my opposition— on the contrary, even—to the idea that the deceased person may continue existing in another place. But that supposed existence can become an obstacle to the mechanism that allows us to develop a new internal relationship with the deceased, which is one of the final steps in the grieving process. Whatever happens in a séance with a medium, whether the deceased is alive *somewhere* or not, they are no longer in an objective external relationship. We don't see them anymore, we don't touch them. The relationship has become subjective. If the grieving person, through what the medium tells them, continues to think that nothing has really changed and that the deceased is still there just as before, that they are able to visit them the way we visit a neighbor or a grandmother, this is not helpful in the long term. Consulting with a medium may also help the grieving process as much as it hinders it; it will really depend on what we are expecting from it. It can be beneficial if the experience leads the grieving person to envision the possibility that there is a continuity of the consciousness and if this possibility brings them relief: "We are not separated forever but I have my own path and my own journey of grief." These two ideas are not incompatible.

Grieving is an emotional process, and I have never heard someone tell me that going to see a medium made a radical and definitive impact on their suffering. This is because, concretely, the deceased person is no longer here. Even if we subscribe to the idea that they might continue living elsewhere, in everyday life my husband, my wife, my child, or my parents are no longer here. It's the vacations all by yourself, the weekends without him or her. This deceased person is genuinely no longer in my world and my process of grief is my response to this wound, to this amputation caused by loss.

I sometimes hear people tell me, astonished: "I went to see a medium, I believe what they told me, but I'm still suffering." Well, yes, that's normal. Going to see a medium with the idea that I'm not going to suffer anymore because I'll know that my deceased loved one exists somewhere else is an illusion. This doesn't change the suffering caused by their daily absence, the fact that I have to live my life, construct and reinvest in activities. This is why I ask my patients about their expectations when they share their desire to see a medium with me. When they say, "If there's something after death, I'll stop suffering." No, you won't. Even if the séance leads to contact and you have the conviction that life continues, something has been broken. The objective tie to reality has been cut and the process of grieving consists very simply of the formation of a scar over this gaping wound, without which you would not be able to hold on psychologically.

So in what way can consulting with a medium be positive if it is not going to stop a person's suffering?
If it can lead a person to consider the possibility that there is a continuity of consciousness after death. This indicates that the separation is not definitive, the rupturing of the

bond is not irreparable. It may also be a way, for some people, to make the suffering easier to accept, since the separation will have an end when, after their own death, they will find the deceased person again. For me as a psychiatrist, I always have the fear that after this kind of contact people will want to accelerate their own death so they can see their loved one. Those things are always complicated to manage, but I am always astonished by the messages received during these so-called contacts. For example, I heard people report to me more than once that during their contact with the deceased person they had been told, "If you kill yourself, you will never find me." I love hearing that because even if my psychological arguments to convince people to not want to die and to live their lives are powerful, they are not the same as words supposedly spoken to these grieving individuals by their disappeared loved ones.

So, yes, the idea that we will see each other later is a belief, but we all live with a multitude of beliefs. Someone will live with the belief that he is worthless, that he's not up to snuff, that he's not worthy of being loved, and living one's whole life with that belief is extremely dangerous psychologically. There are people who will live by the belief that they will never be successful in life, that they're not very interesting. All of those things are just beliefs, and we subscribe to them heavily without questioning them. We live with them. Thinking that there is a life after death is a belief, and whether I agree or not has an effect on my behavior. If I am convinced of the continuity of the consciousness, this belief may lead some people to consider their behavior, and in this way their actions in the world are not completely devoid of meaning. It's Pascal's wager: if there is something afterwards, one might as well do good things that will have continuity after death. It's fairly reasonable.

Could belief in life after death make us more fragile?
For me, the only danger is one of addiction. The process of grieving will not be interfered with if there is not an obsession with maintaining the link. But some people do indeed consult every medium possible and are on the lookout for the slightest sign. This could prove to be very harmful. First of all, because we spend a lot of energy trying to reestablish the bonds we have lost. Second, because in trying to make an external relationship last as if the person were still present, we block the proper sequence of the process of grieving, which consists of, as I said, an interiorization of this bond in order to continue living one's own life without the disappeared loved one. The multiplication of hypothetical contacts with the deceased can clearly prevent the person grieving from advancing and reinvesting in their life. They are no longer anchored in reality. In fact, good mediums refuse to see people with that kind of regularity, and only accept one or two consultations per year with the same person. This, I would say, is a measure of their honesty.

What would be the right attitude to adopt when speaking with a medium?
First of all, be aware of the state of mind you are in. See yourself as you are: you are full of enormous expectations, and be realistic about the fact that this dramatically skews what you will be told. Secondly, be aware that you are across from a human being who, even if they claim to be in contact with the beyond, will act as a filter. Therefore, whether or not there is contact, this filter will appear in what is said. The subjectivity of the medium—their wounds, their own beliefs—will be present. You also need to be careful not to take objectively what you are receiving subjectively via the intermediary of

this person who says something is "going through them." Because you are not the one in direct contact; it's someone else, and you have to think about everything arbitrary that that might entail.

Yes, be aware of your expectations, of your vulnerability, of your desire to believe that you really are receiving a message from your brother, your mother, your husband. Know that you are in a situation where objectivity is lost and that the information that is reaching you is not coming to you in a protected space that you are used to.

Could you return to the idea of addiction in the relationship that certain people maintain with mediums?
If there is actual contact with the beyond, and if the beyond exists, we can imagine that the deceased have other things to do apart from responding to endless solicitations from the person who is grieving. They must find this greatly troubling, and it must significantly hinder their personal development. I often use the example of a child who is leaving to study on the other side of the world and his mother who wants to contact him every five minutes by phone, email, or text: it will then be impossible for the child to live calmly and grow. This is the image I am trying to convey. If this obsession endures, there may need to be some psychological work done on this attachment. We are now looking at a profile of addiction and we try, as with every addiction, to make the person aware of it. If the person says that it's good for them, it's a bit like they're saying that drinking relaxes them but no, they're not an alcoholic, they just drink two bottles of wine and that relieves their anxiety. How can we help a person let go of a toxic link that *they* think is beneficial to them? The person is operating in an emotional field, so we need to try to lead

them to a mental, cognitive level with words, and show them that this addiction is harmful to the harmonious progression of their grieving process. Even if their addiction helps them at one level, it keeps them stuck in one step of the process, the continuation of which is constantly being postponed.

But the presence of deceased people in another world is a reality for billions of human beings and has been for millennia. Isn't a grieving process that no longer considers a deceased loved one as being on the exterior an arbitrary secular idea?

No, the two ideas are not incompatible. We talk about a psychological process of grieving that helps us restore the external and objective bond that has been broken. This is done through the slow process of introjecting the bond, which leads us to feel that we carry that person within us. People say, "He's inside me." That's the psychological process of grieving, and it's not at all incompatible with the existence of another more spiritual dimension at the same time. The process of grieving is a psychological mechanism. How do we cope? Its purpose is to ease the suffering by replacing an experience of separation with an experience of intimate presence. This intimate and internal bond is not at all incompatible with a possible connection to another dimension. The subjective feeling that is built during the process of grieving is part of the same territory as this spiritual link.

Appendix

If You Are Interested in Consulting a Medium

Anyone who is grieving and wants to see what the experience is like should respect certain rules to protect themselves and defend against abuses that may lead to additional suffering in a period when they are already made vulnerable by their grief.

1. To reduce the chance that the individual presenting themselves as a medium draws information from the psyche of the grieving person rather than from the beyond, the person consulting them should not provide any details about the deceased, not even their name, gender, age, or how they are related to them. The individual should simply tell the medium that they would like to obtain information about a deceased person. A confident medium who is convinced of their power to truly communicate with the deceased will not need additional instructions. They will be convinced that the deceased will enter into contact with them to transmit any useful information. A photo may be necessary for some mediums to facilitate the connection, though. You should not be asked for any other details.

2. Once the contact with the deceased seems to have been made, the medium will say that they have received a message that they would like to clarify or have validated by the person consulting them: "What does that mean? Why is the deceased showing me this?" Here again, the person consulting should provide as little information as possible, responding, for example, that they understand or don't understand the message, without revealing any recognizable symbols or references to the medium.

3. The consultant may answer, at no risk, only the following question: with what I have told you up until now, does it seem to you that I was contacted by the person you wanted to hear from? The answer can be summarized with a simple yes or no, without any additional explanation.

So, if you would like to see a medium, give as little information as possible. When you arrange a meeting, don't give your last name. Provide minimum details during the séance and you will see if the medium is trying to read you to find information or if they are making statements that are so general that they could apply to anyone. Think about the logical deductions the medium may be able to make just by looking at you, by looking at the photo or photos of the deceased that you brought, or by listening to you, and keep those in mind so you are not too amazed by the so-called revelations.

Remember that grief alters our perception of reality at every level. Our need to contact the deceased is so strong that we have a tendency to think that communication is happening even when the medium is a fake. Protect yourselves psychologically, use this experience constructively, and it may help you. Talk about what the medium told you with your family or an open-minded third party (a therapist, a psychologist, etc.). Finally, your actions should not depend on what a medium tells you.

Acknowledgments

This book was made possible most of all by the participation of mediums who trusted me in spite of the stress and the strain I put them through. I would like to express my immense gratitude to them for having been willing to lay themselves bare as they did.

This book would also have been impossible without the involvement of my father, who from *somewhere else* made the effort to collaborate with me on it, probably filled with the hope, as I was, that these pages might bring a little relief to the people who are as afraid of death as he was when he was alive.

Thank you to the other deceased, Louis, Lise, and Paul, and all of those known and unknown to me who took part in this adventure.

Thank you also to my mother Claude and my brother Simon for allowing me to reveal, in these pages, the sometimes intimate details of our family for the purpose of illuminating more clearly the way that a séance with a medium unfolds.

Thank you to my friend Christophe Fauré, for whom I have an immense admiration. With his enormous heart and unbelievable professionalism, Christophe helps a great number of people live better lives during the small and large trials that they face. Both in consultation and through his books, Christophe is a good man.

Thank you to Sébastien Lilli, my partner from the beginning at INREES, and the current president of the institution we built together. By fully taking the reins of this adventure, and with a skillful hand, you allowed me to have the time to complete this book.

Thank you to all of the employees, journalists, and volunteers at INREES, without whom this adventure would not have been possible, those who were there from the first hour and those who are joining us today. We form an amazing family, and I feel immensely proud to work with all of you.

Thank you to Agnès Delevingne, who for years has supported and led the network of volunteer psychologists at INREES. Her energy and talent now allow people going through complicated experiences to find, at no cost, a source of support and a listening ear.

Thank you also to the volunteers in the INREES health professionals network, who never withhold their time or their energy. You are doing pioneering work of tremendous importance. I admire your devotion.

Thank you to my editor, Marc de Smedt, for having believed so strongly in this book, and for having supported it from the beginning. Feeling your confidence and enthusiasm carried me through.

Thank you to Albin Michel and its president Francis Esménard for their continued confidence in me for this third book together. Every book is important to an author, and to have such a prestigious publishing house promoting my work in such a beautiful way is of immeasurable worth.

Thank you to Marie-Pierre Coste-Billon, who has supported me with such thoughtfulness and professionalism since my arrival at Albin Michel. One of life's strange little ironies: Marie-Pierre was a student of my father's.

ACKNOWLEDGMENTS

Thank you to Hélène Ibanez, who corrected this manuscript with unbelievable talent and extraordinary respect, chasing away my typos and numerous spelling mistakes, and whose suggestions were indispensable.

Thank you to Albin Michel's foreign rights director Solène Chabanais for her dedication to have this book translated in several countries.

Thanks to Lucinda Karter from The French Publishers' Agency in New York for receiving me with such warm enthusiasm.

Thanks to my publisher in the United States, Tony Lyons, founder of Skyhorse Publishing, Inc. I'll long remember our first, nearly three-hour meeting during which I was able to present my work and my journey in these unexplored fields. Thank you for your trust and confidence.

Specials thanks to Grace McQuillan for her work, her respect of my text, and her delicate way of translating my words and those of the mediums . . . and my father's.

Thanks to my editors Andrew Geller and Chamois Holschuh at Helios Press and all the wonderful team at this marvelous independent publisher.

I would not be the man I have become without my wife, Natacha Calestrémé. We have shared our existence for many years, and growing old together is a profound source of joy and fulfillment. The two of us are already a little like one person. Thank you for your patience and your kindness in every moment.

Thank you to my daughter Luna, whom I love more than everything in the world. You probably felt as though your father was a little too involved in his work, and I want to thank you today for your kindness and respect. You are a woman I admire deeply. This book is for you more than anyone else.

I want to end by thanking, from the bottom of my heart, Véronique Dimicoli, who assisted me throughout the phases of the test and interviews. With an unparalleled professionalism, availability, and kindness, Véronique helped me by transcribing dozens of hours of recording and by sharing her questions with me, which were always pertinent. Your help has been monumental. Thank you, Véronique.

For more information or to write the author, go to:
www.inrees.com

Stéphane Allix is the founder of the Institute for Research on Extraordinary Experiences (INREES), which studies seriously the subjects we term *supernatural*. At a time when new fields of knowledge are emerging, INREES offers a context in which to discuss science, spirituality, and the latest research on the consciousness, life, and death, and brings the visible and invisible worlds closer together in a scientific and thorough manner. No taboo, no prejudice, only rigor and openness.

The site www.inrees.com is today's most extensive online source of information in the French language, gathering in one place all of the scientific publications available on the subject, including previously unseen articles, videos, and all of the latest extraordinary things, because it is possible to be interested in the things that we cannot explain all while keeping two feet on the ground.

Stéphane Allix also founded *Inexploré*, a reference magazine for the general public on the frontiers of psychology, spirituality, and the sciences. Available at newsstands or by subscription (www.inrees.com).